To James
always the "Best"
for you. God bless you,
Anne Howard

ALL THINGS
HIDDEN

One Woman's Story of Betrayal
and Redemption

D1452580

ALL THINGS
HIDDEN

*One Woman's Story of Betrayal
and Redemption*

anne flowers

All Things Hidden

One Woman's Story of Betrayal and Redemption

ISBN 0-88144-007-8

Copyright © 2006 by Anne Flowers

10026-A South Mingo Road #296

Tulsa, OK 74133

Dedication

I dedicate this book to the two Roberts in my life, Robert Flowers and Admiral Robert Fulton. Both have shown me incredible love and loyalty as long as I have known them.

And to the many friends who have encouraged me along the way, like Dean, Ella, Virginia, Big Mama, Joy, Jim and Brenda, Beth and Craig, Peter, Jerome, Gladys, Bill, Carol, Iris, my Aunt Nancy, and so many others. Thank you so much for your love.

I would like to thank those ministries whose teaching tapes and television programs gave me hope and encouragement when I was a new Christian and struggling to survive in that little, old apartment. To Marilyn Hickey, Kenneth and Gloria Copeland, Charles Stanley, and James and Betty Robison—you laid a foundation in my life that has seen me through every trial and trouble. Thank you for being so faithful!

Table of Contents

Author's Note

This is my story. I have told the truth and described the events of my life as I saw them, as I experienced them, as I felt them. No doubt there will be those who strongly disagree with my view of some of these events, but again, this is my side of the story. I will venture to say that anyone who considers my point of view may find their eyes and understanding opened in a startling manner.

When we get to heaven (those of us who actually do get to heaven), God can straighten all of us out on the points that were skewed by our human faults and failings. In the meantime, this is how I see it.

Therefore judge nothing before the time,
until the Lord come,
who both will bring to light the hidden things of darkness,
and will make manifest the counsels of the hearts:
and then shall every man have praise of God.

1 Corinthians 4:5
The Holy Bible, King James Version

CHAPTER 1

DAWN OF RECOGNITION

The light began to dawn in 1962 when my grandmother died. She was my mother's mother, and I had never known her at all. I understood that I had visited her one time in Lexington, Mississippi, for two or three days when I was a little bitty girl. But I had no recollection of it. In fact, I knew nothing about my mother's family except some names that were mentioned from time to time. This was due to the fact that my parents had been divorced when I was a baby, and I had grown up under my father's care.

My husband Grey and I had just returned from a weekend of Mardi Gras partying in New Orleans. Monday morning had come all too soon to our large household, especially since I was very pregnant. Somehow I had awakened and dressed and managed to get the children up and dressed. Ella, who was far more than just a maid to us, had arrived and wonderful aromas were calling us to breakfast.

Ella watched the younger children while I took the older ones to school. When I returned, she had a delicious cup of coffee waiting for me, and I took it straight to our bedroom. I heard the shower running, which told me Grey was up. Putting the cup of coffee on my bedside table, I slipped off my shoes and crawled back into bed. I fluffed up the pillows and picked up the newspaper. I always read the last part of the paper before the first. In fact, I always read the stock market and then skipped the sports and went to the front page. That morning, however, my glance fell on a name in the obituaries. I don't usually read that section, but I happened to see it. So God had something in mind. The small headline read, "Elizabeth Glass Busick Jones Sullivan."

I thought, *Those names are very familiar.* I knew they were on my mother's side. So I called my father, read the obituary to him, and asked him, "Daddy, is this, could this be my grandmother, the grandmother I never knew?"

He said, "Yes, Honey, it is." He paused and then went on to say, "Of course Elizabeth, your mother, will be at the funeral, and her sister, your Aunt Nancy."

"Should I go? I don't know any of them." I was seized with the anxiety that comes from too many unknown factors.

"I wish you would go, Anne," he said. "Lizzy was such a sweet, pretty, and loving woman. I was always very fond of her." He added. "I'll write Elizabeth immediately. She and Nancy loved their mother. They took care of her and also their Aunt Annie for years. Please go. I think it's important, Anne. I think it's important for you. They would appreciate it because they were so close to Lizzy."

He always called my grandmother Lizzy.

"But Daddy, I'm scared," I said.

"You can do it, Honey," he said.

My father had always said to me, "You can do it, Honey."

And, as always, a rush of adrenaline ran through my body. I hung up the phone and decided. I would go! This would be an adventure. But first I had to ask Grey to go with me. When I thought of that, I felt uneasy again. I walked over to the bathroom door and called out, "Grey, I think my grandmother's dead. I think it's my mother's mother."

I read the obituary to him and he called back, "Well, have you called the Colonel?" Hearing Grey refer to my father in this manner added to my anxiety. I remembered how my life had changed so drastically the day my father was called into military service during World War II. I was just twelve when he was summoned to the White House to meet with President Roosevelt. Then he was gone for extended periods of time, and no explanation was given to us about what he was doing or where he was going. This was difficult and often frightening to me.

I brought my mind back to the task at hand, shook off my fears, and called out, "Grey, the funeral is at eleven o'clock downtown. Will you take me?"

He replied, "No, I can't do that. I have something to do at the office. But I'll meet you there." I was relieved that he said he would be there, but something in his voice caused me to remain apprehensive. Deep down I didn't trust him to keep his word, but I desperately wanted to.

My uneasiness stemmed not only from not being sure of Grey but also from facing an entire part of my family with whom I was totally unfamiliar. I really didn't want to go alone. Although I had never heard anything but the most glorious, loving things about my mother and her family from my father, she and her side of the family were complete strangers to me.

I thought, *How can I do this? How will I know which one is my mother?*

Grey dressed and left for his office. I tried to put myself at ease by going about my morning routine. When it was time I left our small children in Ella's care to get ready. I pulled a nice dress over my rotund middle, something appropriate for a funeral. The services were to be held at Wright & Ferguson on High Street there in Jackson, and the graveside burial service would be in Brandon, Mississippi. That's where my grandmother's family came from, about twenty miles east of Jackson.

I had a lot of questions and a sense of panic as I drove toward High Street. While I was growing up, other children would say they were going to grandmother's house for Thanksgiving, or they were seeing their grandparents on Sunday or something like that. I never understood what they were talking about because I didn't have grandparents in my life. I often wondered what it would be like to have them. Sometimes it shook me up when anyone spoke the words—grandmother, grandfather, grandparents—because it made me feel like I was missing something important.

The parking lot was nearly full, and I was surprised there was such a big crowd. I shouldn't have been because in the South everybody is connected and my grandmother had been a very wealthy woman besides. Since I was raised mostly in Washington, D.C., and New York City, funerals in the South were fascinating and a little unnerving to me. Laying loved ones to rest was a festive gathering time for relatives and friends who didn't see each other except on such occasions.

They didn't celebrate the death; they celebrated seeing each other, and funerals were more like parties with plenty of food and drink.

I parked the car and looked for Grey's. It wasn't there, so I walked slowly toward the chapel feeling very alone. Grey had said he'd be there, and I was hurting with disappointment that he wasn't. Once inside, I asked for directions. "Upstairs, third parlor on the left," they said. Being seven months pregnant, climbing the stairs left me slightly winded, and I was glad when I reached the top.

The sign at the large entrance to the third parlor had my grandmother's name on it. My heart was pounding. I saw men and women standing around, chatting. Some were sitting and fanning and talking. I didn't know any of these people. None of them looked familiar. None of them even looked like me— but one of these women was my mother.

To my right a line had formed with about twelve or fifteen people moving toward a large alcove that contained the casket. I could see that when people got to the alcove, they turned right before walking past the casket. My relatives were probably in there, behind the wall, and I wouldn't see them until I turned that corner.

The line moved steadily and soon I was at the alcove. I turned the corner. The casket was to my left but I didn't look at it. My eyes were riveted on the people I was approaching. In a few moments I would see my mother and perhaps Aunt Nancy—whoever they were. We kept moving closer and closer to the receiving line, but I still couldn't see anyone that I recognized.

I tried to remember what my mother looked like. The last

time I had seen her was for a few fleeting moments when I was twelve, during the war. My father had taken my sister and me to the Mayflower Hotel in Washington, D.C., where she was staying. We all had lunch together, then a chauffeur took us back home. That dim memory was not much help now.

Finally I was just two people away. I saw a beautifully dressed lady and instantly knew it was her. When I reached her, I put my hand out and said, "I'm Anne Sharp."

Her eyes twinkled with her brilliant smile and she immediately hugged me. She said, "Darlin', I'd know you anywhere." She was poised and at ease, and I was completely the opposite. I was pregnant, nervous, and frustrated that my husband hadn't shown up to support me.

I didn't meet Aunt Nancy at that time. My mother had other people to receive and encouraged me to go on and view my grandmother. She said warmly, "Baby, be sure you look at Ma." I walked on with the line, but I didn't look at the casket. Later I realized that I had missed an opportunity to see what my mother's mother looked like. At that time I had never seen a picture of her.

As I was leaving the alcove, the funeral director came in, went over to my mother, and said, "It is time for the service." Still no Grey. As I moved into the main room, I didn't know what to do.

Just then my mother came over and said, "Anne Sharp, you must sit with me." The casket was taken out, and the funeral director said he would come back for us. Just then my sister and her husband came in. It was at this point that my mother introduced me to Aunt Nancy. My mother's half sister was young. I guessed she was probably in her early forties—about ten years older than I was—and I liked her instantly. She was very warm.

The funeral director came back for us and took us downstairs to the anteroom of the chapel, where we could view the service without being seen. As we sat down, Grey Flowers entered with great fanfare and concern, not for me but for *my mother*. I was sitting on her left and he sat on her right. I thought that was odd and was hurt because it seemed he was not there for me. He was just trying to impress my relatives.

After the service Grey insisted on driving my mother to the gravesite. He escorted her downstairs, while I followed behind. I sat next to her in the back seat of his newly washed Cadillac. Aunt Nancy sat in front with Grey. My mother commented to me about how thoughtful and charming he was. At the gravesite she pointed out her various family members and told me all about them. I was introduced to all the headstones who were my relatives. Then we went to a relative's house, where she introduced me to more of my family. They were very gracious and genteel but not gregarious. The food was plentiful but not lavish, and only immediate family members were present. To my relief, this was not the typical Mississippi funeral celebration.

I saw photographs of my great grandparents, grandparents, aunts, uncles, and cousins I had never met. I knew I wanted to know more about them. Grey was very excited to be included in all this and was the perfect gentleman. After lunch my mother and Aunt Nancy told us that they were leaving very early the next morning and wouldn't be able to see us the next day, so we said our good-byes. Grey and I drove back to get my car at the funeral home, then he went to his office and

I returned home—with a very strange feeling inside.

The following weekend Grey and I went to a cocktail party. I overheard a brief exchange between Grey and the man who had been the best man at our wedding. He asked Grey, "What was Anne's mother like?"

Grey replied, "I'll put it to you this way, Dick, if she walked into a crowded room, every head would turn in her direction."

When I heard this, it was as though somebody was trying to pull a thick curtain from my eyes. Deep inside I sensed betrayal, that there were things Grey had not told me. But I could not imagine what they could be. So I quickly dismissed the whole matter.

CHAPTER 2

A SAD LOVE STORY

My father, Allison Ridley Williams, was a dashing bachelor of thirty-three years when he met my mother. A very wealthy contractor in Mississippi, he had graduated from Massachusetts Institute of Technology and had taken courses at Harvard and Princeton as well. Although born a Southerner, he was one year old when his family moved to Washington, D.C.

My father's family were very politically active. His great-great-grandfather, his great-grandfather, and his father all served in Congress. His father, John Sharp Williams, was elected to the United States House of Representatives when Daddy was a year old, and so he grew up in our nation's capital in the world of politics. After a number of terms in the House and serving as minority whip, my grandfather was elected to the Senate then later became the minority leader. He was never defeated in an election and served over thirty years.

My father's family lived in a big, white house where the Supreme Court now stands, and my grandfather would walk across the street to the Capitol to go to work. However, my father's path was not to be political, although he had many contacts and worked with politicians through the years.

After high school Daddy served in the army during World War I. He achieved the rank of captain, a very young captain at that. After the war and schooling, he formed a construction company in Mississippi and built electric plants and such. He was a catch in Mississippi, but he was also a catch in the Northeast, especially in Boston. I have some letters from Honey Fitzgerald, the mayor of Boston, to my grandfather. Honeyfitz, as he was called, had contacted my grandfather, who was minority leader of the Senate at the time, and requested that my father escort his daughter Rose to her debut.

I have pictures of Rose Fitzgerald and other debutantes of the time with my father. It was obvious that he enjoyed them, but he was never serious about any of the young ladies. As we all know, Rose Fitzgerald married Joe Kennedy, but my family's acquaintance with the Kennedys continued when I was twenty. I met one of their sons and his first cousin when we all sailed with a group of young people to Europe. We were on the USS America, and he and I won a dance contest! He was a very nice boy when I knew him, a really sweet, shy, delightful young man.

Although my father could have married just about any woman he wanted, he stayed a bachelor until he saw my mother. He met her when he attended a dance at Belhaven College in Jackson, Mississippi, with my mother's Aunt Mary. At the time Belhaven was a girl's finishing school, and my mother was a student there.

My mother, Elizabeth Busick Jones, was almost orphaned as a child. Her father died when she was about six months old. She was taken to live with her grandmother in Brandon, Mississippi, and I believe her mother took her brother to St. Louis. Later they would become reacquainted, but for the most part she grew up with her grandmother and seven uncles.

My mother's grandmother was a very wealthy woman, probably the wealthiest woman in the state at the time. Her uncle and grandfather had owned railroads, cotton gins, and had farmed cotton on over forty plantations since the Civil War. At one time it was said that Uncle Ned Richardson controlled more cotton than the Emir of Egypt. Needless to say, my mother had everything she wanted. By the time she was sent to Belhaven College, however, her grandmother was very ill. My mother loved her grandmother dearly, and it was during this difficult time in her life that my father walked in to a tea dance—as her Aunt Mary's escort.

As my father danced with Mary, he looked across the room and saw this magnificent young girl. She was about five feet six inches tall, had a near perfect figure, blue eyes that were large and expressive and framed by long lashes, and beautiful medium-blonde hair. She was an extremely graceful dancer, and her laugh was captivating. He said, "I have got to meet her. I want to marry her." The aunt was not pleased but did as he asked, and so my parents met.

When my father asked her to dance, my mother was captivated by him as well. He was handsome, successful, and the son of U.S. Senator John Sharp Williams. Close to six feet tall and tan from being outdoors, his almost violet-blue eyes were framed with long, thick lashes that matched his chestnut hair. He was a terrific dancer, so all this and his fancy red roadster completely swept my mother off her feet. He was everything she could ever want—except for one thing. She told me later that she had thought, *This is ridiculous. He's too old. He's an old man.*

Shortly after the tea dance, my mother's grandmother's illness worsened. Of course, when she learned of Allison Williams' interest in her granddaughter, she wanted them to marry immediately. This would ensure Elizabeth's future financially and socially. It was very hard for my mother. She was only fifteen and the one person she had always relied upon was dying.

My mother felt that there was no one she could turn to but my father. Her mother was not someone she could count on at that time. She had remarried a Mr. Sullivan and lived in another state, and that union produced my mother's only sister, Nancy. So Elizabeth Jones married Allison Williams on August 25, 1925, and turned sixteen in early December. My father did not know that she was only fifteen when he married her. Her mother and grandmother had lied about her age on the marriage certificate, believing a bachelor in his early thirties would never marry a girl of fifteen.

They went on a long, extended honeymoon, and my father introduced my mother to the joys of love, marriage, and travel. My mother didn't want to go to Europe; she just wanted to see the eastern United States and Canada. She had grown up reading *The New Yorker* magazine and had always dreamed of leaving Mississippi. So they traveled for months, mostly in private cars on trains.

Years later, when my mother and I became reacquainted, she told me that their first stop had been Chicago. They stayed at the Drake Hotel, and on the first night she spent with my father, after she had gotten ready for bed, she did what her grandmother had taught her always to do. She knelt by the bed, folded her little hands, and said her prayers.

My father walked out of the bathroom to find his young teenage bride sweetly praying out loud. It intimidated and unnerved him! My mother told me that for the first four or five nights, she would pray by the bed, climb into bed next to him, kiss him goodnight, and quickly turn away from him. Pulling the covers up to her chin, she would then go to sleep. After several nights of this, however, she realized that something more should be happening. So the next night she didn't turn away.

After the marriage was finally consummated, my father was so ecstatic that he rushed downstairs and woke up the hotel manager so he would open up the jewelry store. To my mother's delight, he came back to their room and showered her with all kinds of beautiful jewelry.

After the honeymoon they returned to Yazoo City, Mississippi, where they were met by Senator and Mrs. Williams and other members of Daddy's family. Elizabeth was overwhelmed with attention. The next morning a bouquet of roses from the Senator welcomed her to her new home, which Daddy had built for her before they were married. It was a two-story white house on Grand Avenue. The Senator was very fond of this pretty young girl and made every effort to make her feel a part of the family. He often sent her flowers and gave her money, mischievously telling her not to tell her husband.

My sister Betty was born there, and then they moved to Jackson because Daddy had obtained a big contract to put in all the streets in what was then called North Jackson. When I met my mother again in 1984, she asked me to take her there. She pointed to a house on Pinehurst Street and said, "You were conceived in that upstairs bedroom." That house was really something. It was the only one in the entire area that had a Florida look about it, with a tiled roof and stucco that was pale pink-orange. Every other house was colonial.

And then she told me a curious story. It happened while they were living in that house and before she became pregnant with me. Being just eighteen, one day she climbed up into an apple tree in the front yard. She was enjoying the view and fine weather when my father arrived with one of his business acquaintances to seal a new contract. When he didn't find her in the house, he and the other man came out the front door and he called, "Elizabeth, where are you?"

She laughed merrily and shouted, "I'm up here!"

My father looked up, saw her in the tree, and became furious. He ordered her to come down, and when she complied, he popped her on the fanny in front of the businessman. Mother went into the house totally humiliated.

They did not live there long before they moved back to the Grand Avenue home in Yazoo City, where I was born two months later. Unfortunately, trouble worse than the apple tree episode erupted in the marriage prior to my birth.

Before my parents married, he was quite the ladies' man. I'm sure he had every intention of becoming monogamous with my mother, but old habits die hard. When my mother was pregnant with me, she walked down the stairs of their home in the middle of the night to find my father in the arms of Aunt Mary, the same aunt who had introduced them at the Belhaven dance!

The sight of my father in the arms of another woman—especially her aunt—devastated my mother. He was the only man she had ever loved, and she had given herself completely to him. She trusted him implicitly. Because he was so much older, he was father, best friend, and lover to her. He was the center of her world, but now she was faced with the reality that she was not the center of his world.

My mother was also a stunning young woman, who drew attention wherever they went. Trips to Chicago and New York had ignited a desire to travel in her, as she was seeing a world she had always dreamed of experiencing. It was difficult for her to be so young and have one baby and another on the way, but her love for my father had kept her happy and secure and given her the desire to be a good wife and mother. After witnessing my father with her aunt, however, all that shattered.

When I was four months old we moved to Memphis, Tennessee, because Daddy obtained some big contracts there. His younger brother was in law practice in Memphis, and he had a wife and three children. Daddy bought a beautiful, large home for us in Chickasaw Gardens on Iroquois Street. It was a lovely English-style, two-story brick home, but the beautiful new surroundings did not mend the tremendous hurt and disillusionment in my mother. She soon told my father, "I've got to leave. I can't stay."

It was then that my father made the first of several bad

decisions. He decided to send my mother to Europe to pursue her education. I suppose this was his way of trying to ease his conscience and make it up to her. She studied art, decorating, and theater at the Sorbonne in Paris. She was so beautiful that she soon became a highly successful model. My Aunt Nancy told me that at one time my mother was one of the highest paid models in Europe and the United States, representing products like Coca Cola and Lucky Strike cigarettes. Eventually she became a successful fashion designer and businesswoman.

With my mother away, my father went to his sister-in-law and said, "Would you take the children?"

My Aunt Gladys said, "I'll take the baby, but I can't take the older one." So he moved my aunt and uncle and cousins into the house he had bought for us just so they could care for me, and he took my older sister with him to New York.

Uncle Kit and Aunt Gladys put my little crib right in their bedroom, and when I cried they would just put me in bed with them. I fit right into their family, and I was very happy there. They were loving and we had lots of fun. From the beginning, I was very easygoing.

While my mother was in Europe, lawyer friends convinced my father to divorce her for desertion and get custody of my sister and me. Discouraged by waiting so long for her to come home, he reluctantly gave in to their relentless prodding. Later on he would say, "She was way too young and I should not have divorced her. I should have given her time to grow up. I should have waited for her to come back." My mother learned of the divorce when she was en route to New York from Europe. She was sailing home for a visit. Distraught, she threw her beautiful wedding band in the ocean, but she had enough good sense to keep the diamond! Although she had been deeply hurt by my father, she turned another page in her life and moved on.

The divorce of my parents was finalized, and my father gained legal custody of Betty and me. It happened while I was living with my aunt and uncle. I was a little over two years old when my father came to get me. Since I was young and an easygoing kid, it wasn't very hard for me, but it was for my cousins. Aunt Gladys told me when I was older that Kit Junior had been pretty upset. He always liked to put me on his bike when he rode around the neighborhood with all his friends. When I left, he sat on the curb and cried.

My father and I traveled by train to New York. Later I heard stories that he was afraid that the difference in the weather would make me sick, so he put two coats on me. He had plenty to do to care for me, but there were many ladies on the train that were willing to help this very handsome single father.

When we arrived in New York, my father had hired a governess for my sister Betty and me. The governess, my sister, and my mother—who had just returned from Europe—met us at the train station. It was difficult for my sister because she had had my father all to herself, and then suddenly she had to share him with a baby sister. This began a rivalry between her and me that I never fully realized until I was an adult.

My father tried to get my sister and me together with our mother as often as possible when we were small children. He was afraid we would grow up without knowing her. This was important to him because he was from a very close family, and I know he felt responsible for her leaving and the divorce.

These early memories of my mother are like snapshots with blank faces. When we visited her, we spent most of our time with our governess and took long walks.

One particular time we were in Narragansett, Rhode Island, strolling along a sea walk. We passed this beautiful palatial home that was closed down. Later we found out it was Al Capone's. He had a tunnel that went from his downstairs poolroom out to the bay. It seems that if he had problems with his clients or people who didn't like what he was doing, he would fit them with concrete shoes, take them through the tunnel, and dump them in the bay!

Daddy saw to it that we spent the summers at resorts like Narragansett, Newport, Jamestown, places in Maine and Connecticut, and one time in the hot Carolina mountains. During these times he would try to get us together with Mother. I remember she always had a lot of beautiful clothes, and wherever we stayed, she had her own private room, which sometimes was next to ours. She never minded that Betty and I played dress-up in her very expensive clothes, jewelry, and shoes.

I was five years old the last summer we visited with her. I remember she wore eyeshades at night because she slept late in the morning, having been out on a date the night before. She would eat with us in the evening. When the governess, my sister, and I would eat in the dining room at the hotel, she always sat with us. Usually Betty would cut up and Mother would have to send her back to the room with the governess. Then she would sit with me, and we'd finish our meal and talk—but just a little. She would have a cocktail or smoke a cigarette. I remember cigarettes very well and started smoking myself when I was thirteen.

Visits with our mother ended abruptly when I was five We were at Narragansett, and my sister and I walked out onto the long porch of the hotel. We heard a couple, sitting in some rocking chairs, whispering, "Those are her children."

I said, "Betty, did you hear that?"

She said, "Yes."

I asked, "What do they mean?"

Betty answered, "I don't know."

We went back into the hotel and saw a newspaper by the concierge's desk. It caught our eye because on the front page was a big picture of a woman who was badly beaten and unrecognizable. Our governess came over to get us, hurried us back to our room, and said that our father wanted us to go back to New York. Unbeknownst to us, my father had called and paid the hotel manager to buy all the newspapers because the woman on the front page was our mother. But the manager had missed one.

When we got back to New York, our father wasn't there. He was with our mother at the hospital. She had been assaulted and robbed. One evening she had been dressing to go on a date and decided to take some of her expensive jewelry out of the hotel vault to wear. When she heard a knock at the door, she called, "Who is it?"

A male voice answered, "Room service."

Without hesitation she opened the door and two men rushed into her room, slamming the door behind them. One held her while the other grabbed a pitcher of ice and struck her on the back of the head, breaking the pitcher. Then they pulled out a bag of rocks and began beating her hand so they could remove her jewelry. One of the rings they were after was originally owned by Dolly Madison, given to her by her husband, President James Madison. My mother's grandmother was a descendent of Lucy, Dolly's younger sister, and had inherited the ring, and then had given it to my mother.

This was during the Depression and mother was a young, wealthy divorcee, so she was an easy mark for such men. After beating her unconscious and taking her jewelry, they left her for dead. When she finally regained consciousness, she called the hotel desk. They notified the police and an ambulance came immediately, which was not a moment too soon. Her right arm was badly broken, her fingers were broken and bruised, there were lacerations on her head and face, and she had a concussion. When she was able, she identified the men who had robbed her and pressed charges. One of them turned out to be the brother of the attorney general of New York, and both were convicted and imprisoned. None of the jewelry was ever recovered.

While the trial was going on my father moved us from New York to Washington, D.C. He was receiving letters from someone who was threatening to kidnap us if our mother did not withdraw her complaint against these two men. The papers had reported that my mother was a wealthy divorcee who had two little girls. This was after the time of the Lindbergh baby kidnapping, and parents with any kind of wealth were nervous. After he turned the threatening letters over to the FBI, they suggested that he send us away until the trial was over. The next thing we knew, we were on our way with our governess to Benton, Mississippi, to stay with our father's older brother and wife, Uncle John and Aunt Pauline.

Also, as a precaution Daddy drew up papers to make them our legal guardians in case something happened to him.

After the robbery and assault my mother became a stranger to me. As I have mentioned before, I saw her when I was twelve years old, but I can barely remember that luncheon. I believe that my father and mother never stopped caring for each other, even after they married other people. Daddy insisted on sending my mother alimony until his death. And when my father remarried, although he loved my stepmother, it seemed that the image of my mother was always there in the background.

CHAPTER 3

THE LOVE BOAT

When my parents divorced, it was my father's wake-up call. He dove into the responsibility of being a good father and stopped dating altogether. My sister and I became his greatest concern. He was now a consultant, and he traveled extensively, so my older sister Betty and I would go with him. We would travel in two cars. His secretary and bookkeeper would drive one car, which contained his business materials. He would drive the other car, which contained us, our belongings—and our governess.

Henriette Emma Marie LeCorre, whom we called Ettie, had been our governess from the time I came to live with Daddy in New York City. Betty and I were crazy about her, and as the years passed we learned how difficult her life had been. She was born in Brittany, France, in 1907. Her father was blonde and blue-eyed from the North of France, and her mother had the dark, beautiful looks of Southern France. Ettie had the same lovely skin, dark hair, and eyes as her mother. She was very close to her mother and also her little brother, eighteen months younger.

When Ettie was seven, her mother died and her father sent the two children to live with an aunt. It was 1914 and the Kaiser of Germany had begun his march to conquer Europe. World War I began and her father had to go into military service. Two years into the war her father was on furlough from the front and came to visit Ettie and her brother. The war had escalated and many innocent people were being killed. He decided to take the children to a Roman Catholic orphanage, believing that would be the safest place for them. He gave the Church all that he had so they would take good care of his children.

The Church immediately separated Ettie and her brother. They set about educating her brother for priesthood, and Ettie would not see him again until 1959. They put Ettie in a girl's workhouse that had no heat, with watered-down soup and stale bread to eat. Many of the little girls died of tuberculosis, including her best friend Yolanda, who was in the bed next to her. The girls were taken to church every day, forced to kneel with a broom behind their knees, and commanded to pray. Ettie said she often fainted because then she was allowed to go back to the dormitory. The priests and the nuns sexually abused some of the girls, but Ettie never told us whether she was one of them. As a result of this experience, she was always terrified of the Catholic Church.

After the war Ettie's father returned to France without his right leg. He didn't have the money to get his children out of the orphanages, so the Roman Catholic Church would not release them. However, when Ettie was fifteen a former friend of her mother's, a wealthy American woman, came to Europe with her children to spend the summer. She knew about Ettie and set about finding her, eventually locating her in the Catholic orphanage. She paid the Church what they requested and they released Ettie to her.

With the blessing of Ettie's father, this wealthy friend of her mother brought Ettie first to England, where she learned English. At age sixteen Ettie came to America as a companion to the woman's daughter, and they lived in Worcester, Massachusetts. When the woman's daughter went to college, Ettie was nineteen years old. She was dismissed and sent to New York to find another position.

Through an agency Ettie soon secured employment with a Chinese doctor and his wife as governess for their two little boys. When the family returned to China after several years, Ettie went back to the agency. It was at that time, in the early 1930s, that my mother returned from Europe because my father was going to retrieve me from Memphis. My parents agreed that they wanted my sister and me to be reared speaking more than one language and with a knowledge of European manners and etiquette. The latest governess for my sister Betty had quit, and my mother set about to hire another. She contacted the agency that handled Ettie and interviewed her along with some others. With a glowing report, she urged my father to conduct a second interview, and he hired her on my mother's strong recommendation.

When I arrived in New York with my father I was met by my sister Betty, my mother, and Ettie. Shortly after that, my mother returned to Europe and we settled in White Plains, New York—but not for long. Because of my father's consulting business and the difficulty of finding work during the Great Depression, we were on the road constantly, mostly moving back and forth between New York and Washington, D.C. Ettie was always with us, our constant companion.

A nanny just takes care of children, but a governess teaches many things and prepares you for life. Along with academic subjects, Ettie taught us how to behave. Because she was French, we learned everything in that language: geography, history, science, and math. Today I still do math "backwards," just like the French do. My English was learned by ear. It wasn't until my oldest daughter asked me, "Mom, will you help me diagram a sentence?" that I realized I had never studied English grammar.

During one of our stays in Washington, D.C., my father purchased a Cris-Craft yacht. We would move the boat back and forth from New York to Washington as Daddy moved from job to job in his consulting business. My sister was twelve and I was ten when my father received a contract in the Washington, D.C. area. We stayed with Ettie on his yacht, which was docked in Chesapeake Bay. He would come out on the weekends to be with us. It was on one of those weekend visits that my sister and I acquired our stepmother.

The twists and turns of life fascinate me. It was ironic that my mother chose the woman who would become her former husband's wife and her children's stepmother. One night, very late, we were awakened by voices coming from the back deck. We heard my father asking Ettie to marry him, and she kept saying, "No, no. I can't do that. I'm in another class."

Although extremely capable and very lovely, Ettie was a quiet, shy woman. Other than teaching us and disciplining us, she said very little. When we traveled, she would sit in front with Daddy, but because of her background and present circumstances, she thought of herself as a servant. The idea of becoming the mistress of the house was daunting to her, even though she had come to love my father. So she continued to resist his proposal, trying to express her belief that she did not fit in his world.

My sister and I said, "What are we going to do?" We jumped up out of our bunks and ran to the back deck. We grabbed Ettie around her waist and chanted, "You've got to marry Daddy." We weren't going to give her up! It was like the movie, Houseboat, with Cary Grant and Sophia Loren.

My sister and I won, and on Christmas Eve 1940 my father and Ettie married. The ceremony was performed at Cedar Grove Plantation, down in Yazoo County, Mississippi, where my father had sent us on several occasions while he worked. We discovered that in the winter this beautiful and charming plantation home was cold, even though it had many fireplaces and some steam heat. But everything was festively decorated with garlands of green and a huge Christmas tree. Ettie made bridesmaid dresses for Betty and me, which thrilled us. Music played, there was plenty of delicious food, and everyone was happy—everyone but me, that is.

I was worried that Santa would never find the tree this far from New York or Washington, D.C. To make matters worse, I was told that there was no Santa. That was it. I began to cry. Ettie saw me crying and quickly took me aside. She thought that I was upset about the wedding and was delighted to discover the true reason for my distress. She assured me that there were sure to be gifts under the tree for us the next morning.

The wedding took place without a hitch, and then something strange happened. Ettie had always slept in our bedroom, but that night she did not. The next morning we didn't see Daddy and Ettie until long after breakfast. We didn't know what was going on. Then we all got on a train. Now we noticed that Ettie slept in Daddy's cabin. By the time we boarded a big double-decker boat and went on their honeymoon with them, we had figured out that our sleeping arrangements had changed permanently. We also noticed that they had a great big stateroom, but we had a little, tiny double-decker bunkroom.

On the ship Daddy said, "Now children, in the morning we're not going to get up. You just go on into the dining room and get anything you want." And we did. We had a wonderful time. We just ordered anything we wanted. We were very impressed that everybody was in uniform on the ship—and off the ship when we returned to New York. Betty and I didn't realize that war was approaching.

One of my most pleasant memories is when Daddy asked Ettie to marry him on the boat. It was so romantic. But Ettie never changed her behavior toward us. She did not want children, and she made no attempt to be our mother or even a stepmother but continued to act as our governess. Still, I always loved her and was very grateful for everything she taught me.

CHAPTER 4

DADDY

Life with my father was one adventure after another on the road. We had a marvelous time! I loved traveling and still do today. We lived in boarding houses, resorts, and hotels. We met so many fascinating people. I learned to adjust to new situations and people, and I believe that is a good thing. Many people don't go anywhere during their lifetime; and if any change takes place in their lives, they don't know how to handle it.

It's funny how we think. I thought my life was normal. I thought everybody lived like we did. After Daddy thought we were ready to enter school, I actually never finished a full year until I was in my teenage years. Looking back, I see how monumental a task it was for him to take two little girls with him as he traveled, especially during a time when a single father was a novelty.

He was an inventive and highly creative engineer, and he used these abilities to parent and take care of us. During the 1930s there were virtually no motels on the highways and few gas stations. When the two little girls in the back seat of his car had to go to the bathroom, I'm sure he panicked a few times. Little boys could just go to the nearest tree, but not little girls! And if we could get to a gas station, the facilities were an outhouse, complete with spiders. Betty and I would go in hand-in-hand as though we were being sent to the guillotine.

Thus, my father designed one of the first porto-potties for our car. With a jigsaw he cut a round hole in the wooden floorboard of our large green Chrysler limo. Into the hole he fitted a brass top that was similar to a ship's porthole. The carpet was loosely placed over it when the porto-potty was not being used. After that, when we would begin to call out, "Daddy, I have to go!" he would simply reply, "Just pull back the carpet, unscrew the brass fitting, and help yourself, girls."

Daddy had strict rules for traveling. No pencils, scissors, or sharp objects in the back seat. I could play with my doll and Teddy bear, and then he devised another delightful form of amusement. He gave us colorful pieces of cloth and gum, which we would use to make clothes for our dolls or ourselves (only for fun, of course). We would chew the gum and use it to attach the pieces of cloth. It was safe and fun—and time consuming!

He drilled holes in the side of the car and through the back seat and ran strong, khaki-colored straps through them. These were our seatbelts. He strapped us in just in case we stopped suddenly or had the always-eventful blowout. On one occasion on a very bumpy road in Connecticut, we watched a tire go out from the right side of the car, jump a low stone fence, and take off into a pasture. Daddy brought the listing car to a stop, got out, jumped the fence, retrieved the tire, put it back on, and we were on our way to his next consulting job. One of my fond memories is sitting and watching him change a tire in his white linen suit and Panama hat.

Daddy also had strict rules for wherever we stayed, but particularly boarding houses. Most of them had signs out front that said, "No dogs or children." (I always thought it was strange when dogs were mentioned before children.) When that was the case, Daddy would explain his situation and assure the manager that his children would behave like adults, and so we were expected to live up to his part of the bargain.

Although the rules were strict and Ettie always made sure we were well-behaved, life on the road with Daddy was fun. He made everything so interesting. One cold morning when we were in the Blue Ridge Mountains he got us up in the wee hours. It was pitch black outside. We didn't dress, but he and Ettie wrapped us up in our coats, hats, and warm boots and tucked us in the back seat with a blanket. As we slept he drove to an inn, then woke us just in time to see the sun rise. Then we enjoyed a hot country breakfast of ham, biscuits, syrup, hot chocolate, and marshmallows.

Another time, while we were staying at a boarding house, Daddy took us to the circus. I got really excited when I saw people pulling taffy, so the following weekend he decided we should have that experience. He got the cook's permission and mixed a big batch of taffy, then gave Betty and me chunks that we all began pulling. Since we were never allowed in the boarding house kitchen, this was a double treat. We pulled and pulled until Betty and I had taffy all over us. When we were finished he had to put us in the bath and scrub all the sticky stuff off. It was very messy and we had a wonderful time, but we never did it again!

Daddy always wore a coat and tie and often whistled or sang. He had a beautiful voice and would entertain us as we drove down the road. After all, there were no radios, CD or DVD players in those days! He would also teach us math, history, science, and literature. He made learning fun and exciting. I especially liked history and continue to study it today. Daddy knew where and when each battle took place on American soil in every war, who fought who, why they fought, and who won. We were never too rushed to stop at an historical site, museum, or art gallery, and so we traveled through pages of history. We were pioneer home schoolers and did not know it.

Recently, as I was writing this memoir, I came across a box of memorabilia that I had never opened. The first thing I noticed was a dollar bill that had been torn in half. The whole dollar had been sent by my father's mother when Betty and I were very young with the following instruction: "Half for Betty and half for Anne Sharp." When Daddy read that to me, I took the dollar and tore it in two, giving Betty her half. Daddy wrote his mother about this amusing event and told her that he had given each of us a dollar.

The next thing I noticed in the box was a group of envelopes with Daddy's handwriting on them. There were three, and they read: "Anne Sharp's hair, age 8 months." "Anne Sharp's hair, age 4 years old." "Anne Sharp's hair, age 6 years old." Contained in them were clippings of my blonde hair tied with a pink ribbon. Also in the box was my first pair of shoes, which he had carefully wrapped, and two letters. One was a letter he wrote to me when I had forgotten my doll and Betty and I were at a summer resort with Ettie and Mother. He was working in another city. It read in part:

Darling Baby Anne,
    I hope you are so happy and good today. I just know that you are. Say, listen. I wonder if you would mind if I kept Pettit Jean with me until I come up. While I know he would be in safe hands with the conductor, I will not have him with me, and if you were here it would be different because I could see you and talk to you. I can't come up for a while and that means I would like to have Pettit Jean here for a while, if you don't mind.
    A big bushel basket full of precious love for you,
                    Your devoted Daddy Dear

I was five years old and my answer to him was as follows:

Daddy Dear,
    I want to tell you to keep Pettit Jean with you. I love you so much.
                            Anne
        X X X X X X X X X X

I look back on my early years with great love and gratitude that I had a father who cared so deeply for me and gave me a wonderful beginning in life.

CHAPTER 5

POTPOURRI OF
PEOPLE AND PLACES

There were a few times when Daddy took a job that kept him in one place for an extended period of time, thus allowing us to be in school. When this happened in Washington, D.C., during our early years, we attended The Maret School, which was founded by two French sisters named Maret. President Woodrow Wilson had brought them to the United States to educate his daughters. The sisters from Paris decided to make America their home and started their own school.

The Maret School was fashionable and attended by the children of diplomats, congressmen, and other government officials. All education was conducted in French, and later Latin and German were introduced. We said the Lord's Prayer in French and sang the "Marseillaise," the French national anthem, instead of the "Star Spangled Banner." Because Ettie taught us in French, this was no problem for Betty and me. It was only when we attended public school as teenagers that we finally learned the Pledge of Allegiance and the "Star Spangled Banner."

We did not realize at the time how many interesting people we were meeting at the Maret School, and some of them had tragic ends. I remember a young boy whose parents were officials in the German Embassy. Their government called them back to Berlin. We learned later that once back in Germany, this young boy had informed the Nazis that his parents had been sympathetic to the United States. His parents were shot and he was given a medal as a member of the Hitler Youth Corps.

Being so young during the Great Depression and before the war, I was only partially aware of how devastating the Depression was. When the stock market had crashed, much of Daddy's money had crashed with it, and he took work wherever he could. I remember long lines of men waiting for jobs, people begging, and women and children selling fruit, flowers, and anything they could in the streets of New York.

After one particularly cold and difficult winter, before my father married Ettie, his brother John graciously invited us to Cedar Grove for the summer while my father worked. So once again Daddy sent us and Ettie to Cedar Grove Plantation in Mississippi. My memory of this visit is vivid. Better known as "The Sharp Place," it was named after my great-great-grandfather, Colonel John Sharp, who was a hero in the Mexican-American War and a friend to Generals Andrew Jackson and Zachary Taylor and Colonel Jefferson Davis. The plantation was located on a red dirt road between Benton and Canton, Mississippi. It was two miles to Benton and about fifteen miles to Canton. I remember the red dirt road as consisting of light, fluffy, red powder except when it rained and became an angry, slick mess.

My Uncle John had always lived on the plantation and had a lovely wife and daughter. Aunt Pauline had married him with the understanding that each summer he would send her to Texas for a month with her family. Although their daughter, Polly, was married and living in Jackson by this time, Aunt Pauline still went to Texas for a month every summer.

Uncle John, or Uncle "Non" as we called him, wanted to teach us the value of hard work and asked us if we wanted to pick cotton. He guaranteed us the same wages as everyone else, which were higher than any other plantation was paying. We quickly said yes and were certain we would get rich quick.

Very early after breakfast we got into his black, Ford pickup and drove to a nearby cotton field. Uncle Non gave me a huge, long white sack with a shoulder strap. I was seven years old, and it nearly swallowed me. I could hardly drag it behind me. Our cook, Margaret, was already out there "pickin'." She had on a big, wide hat, long sleeves, and a long, full dress. I had on shorts and a shirt. Somehow I knew I was ill prepared.

Margaret showed us how to hold our fingers so we wouldn't cut them on the hard, pointed shells of the open cotton bolls. I began with great enthusiasm, but it was short-lived. I cut and stabbed my fingers on the sharp points and found there was hardly any cotton in my bag after picking and dragging it for what seemed forever. Sweating and fingers bleeding, I must have been a pitiful sight.

I have never been so relieved as when Uncle Non appeared a few hours later to check on us. I ran to meet him and jumped into the truck. All thoughts of getting rich quick were replaced with relief, but as we drove off my admiration and respect for

Margaret and the others was immeasurable. Not only did they skillfully and rapidly pick cotton, but you could hear their beautiful voices singing, laughing, or chattering away.

Margaret was remarkable anyway. She was a champion cotton picker and this was her favorite time of year. She would take time off from the kitchen to pick cotton and visit with friends and family. But she was also an excellent cook. I can still taste her hot biscuits, great sausage, fried green tomatoes, quail, greens, cornbread, and cakes. They were beyond comparison.

At the end of the day the sacks of cotton were weighed in and everyone was paid in cash. I would often go to watch as they emptied the long, heavy sacks into the narrow, wooden wagons. They were like buckboards with high sides. There was one driver named Joseph that I remember. He was big and strong and would climb onto the wagon, take the worn, leather reins in his big hands, and tell the mule, "Git up now!"

The wagons would kick up red dust as they rolled down the dirt road, and we would follow in Uncle Non's truck for the two miles to the Benton Gin Company. Once I rode in Joseph's wagon, sitting on top of the cotton. I thought the ride would be soft and cushy, but it wasn't. There were still some sharp hulls in the cotton, and the seeds were hard. By the time we reached the gin, I was hot and sweaty and streaks of orange-brown perspiration ran down my cheeks. My long, blonde hair was wet, stringy, and a new color!

I jumped down and went around picking up clumps of cotton that had fallen from the loads and gave them to Joseph. "No Missy," he said, "That cotton ain't no good. It's poor. It won't even do fair-to-middlin'." I was disappointed.

They had worked so hard that it hurt me to see anything lost. Joseph saw my expression and said, "Don't you worry, Missy. De Lawd, He know if the bird fall and de Lawd, He know when the cotton fall." That settled it for him and so it settled it for me.

As I look back over my life, there was so much diversity of experience. We experienced life on a cotton plantation but spent most of our growing up in the north. And there were so many occasions that I was in the right city at the right time. We were in Chicago during the 1933 World's Fair. While Daddy worked, Ettie would take us to the Fair. I was very young, but I remember it. When we left the plantation and rejoined our father in New York City, the Great World's Fair of 1939-40 was in full swing. We took the train from Long Island to the Fair nearly every weekend.

After Daddy and Ettie were married in December 1940, we spent some time in New York. Once again adventure came to us. We were living in a boarding house on Long Island. There was a pretty lady on the second floor, and a man with a crew cut often came to pick her up. They always spoke German to each other. My father, who spoke fluent German, picked up on some of their conversations. We had only been there three weeks when Daddy realized that this man was a very high official in the German Nazi Party, also called the Brown Shirts.

My father did not tell anybody at the boarding house, but he notified the FBI. They planted someone there to observe and listen, and a week later Daddy came home and told us that he was going to take us downtown for dinner. We left, and evidently the rest of the boarders were asked to leave. When the man with the crew cut came to pick up the woman that evening, he was arrested and identified as the head of the Nazi Party in the United States. Although an American, I believe he moved to Germany.

We soon left that boarding house and moved to Kew Gardens on Long Island. This is where I met Sammy. He lived up the street, had red hair, and I thought he was cute. It was very cold and snowing outside, but he would come to play with me and the other children on our block. Then one day the other children said, "Anne Sharp, you shouldn't play with Sammy."

I said, "Why?"

They looked at me very matter-of-fact and said, "He's a Jew." I had never heard that word before.

That night at the boarding house I asked Daddy, "What's a Jew?"

He said, "Honey, they're God's chosen people. They're in the Bible." He took out his Bible and read some passages in the Old Testament to me. I didn't understand what he read but I knew it was important. Then he explained that the German Nazis hated the Jews and there was a war going on in Europe because of this hatred. Some man named Hitler with a funny moustache was the bad guy. Daddy would take his little black comb, put it over his upper lip, raise his arm, and say, "Heil Hitler!" I thought he was ridiculous, but he was teaching us a lesson in history—and a lesson in human nature. My father assured me that it was fine for me to play with Sammy, so I continued to do so. But then the bigger teenage boys in the neighborhood started chasing him away. One day they stuffed snow down his snowsuit, calling him a dirty Jew. After that I never saw Sammy again. Even today my heart aches that I was too young to do anything about this terrible injustice. My blood always boils whenever someone is being unfairly or unjustly treated.

In the summer of 1941 we moved to an apartment in Washington, D.C. World War II became the center of activity for us and everyone we knew. We did not realize how much it would affect our new family for a while. Daddy and Ettie decided to take an evening bookkeeping course together. I remember how delighted Daddy was that Ettie received a higher grade than he received. Our joy as a family was short-lived, however, when the war came to our home.

Daddy received a call from his childhood friend, General Brehon Sommerville, who asked him to meet with him and President Roosevelt in the Oval Office. They said, "Allison, we need someone we can trust." At that time Sommerville was a three-star general in charge of the Service Of Supplies (S.O.S.). Thus, by the first part of 1942, Daddy went into the military again and received the rank of colonel. General Sommerville put him in charge of rationing the electrical power to be used in the Manhattan Project. Since this was top secret, my father was the "bad guy" who had to take electricity from different companies and businesses without explanation and funnel it to the Project. Some businesses had to cut down or went out of business because of this. They were very angry with my father, but he could not explain his actions to anyone.

Daddy would come and go and we never asked questions. Later I found out that the Manhattan Project was the code name for the development of the atomic bomb. Only then did I fully understand the challenge my father had faced and why we had to do without him so much during those years.

Life during that time was another adventure to me, despite my father's absences. We lived in a luxurious apartment, complete with a doorman and double lobbies, at 4801 Connecticut Avenue. There was underground valet parking, and we enjoyed a roof garden where we could sit and view the city. Washington was the hub of world events at that time, and our apartment building was in the center of that hub. Fortunately for us, the rents were frozen during the war and we were able to afford this wonderful place. It was not unusual to get on the elevator or walk in the door with someone who had been on the front page of the newspaper that day.

Those I remember are Admirals Bull Halsey, Chester Nimitz, and Hyman G. Rickover; Robert Oppenheimer, chief scientist on the Manhattan Project; League of Nations Representative Ralph Bunch, whose girlfriend lived there; different cabinet members; Senators Eastland, Dirkson, and Stennis; Congressmen McGrant, Abernathy, and Vinson; numerous generals; movie stars who were now in uniform; and many other notable and historical figures.

Vice President Harry S. Truman lived in the apartment building next door. He and his family had lived there during his years as senator from Missouri and now as vice president. At that time the government did not have a special residence for the vice president. This came later. The National Naval Observatory— we used to visit there—was also the site of the home of the Chief of Naval Operations. This home was later refurbished to become the official residence for the vice president. The first vice president to reside there was Vice President Bush.

I remember Mr. Truman as a wonderful, sweet man. He

went walking every day, and in cold weather he would wear a hat and coat. I remember he often had a dog with him and he walked very fast. There were no Secret Service agents around him, and he would play with us. In his backyard there was a little hill where he taught us to play king of the mountain when it snowed. He showed me how to make great snowballs and stack a supply to defend my position on the hill.

On Friday nights we would often see the Trumans at the Uptown and the Avalon movie houses on Connecticut Avenue. Daddy would take us when he was home. It was a great family place, and often we could hear Margaret and her girlfriends chatting during the movie. Then on April 12, 1945, when I came home from school, police cars and the Secret Service were everywhere, and there was black bunting under all the windows of the apartment next door. The Trumans apartment faced Connecticut Avenue.

"Extra! Extra! Roosevelt is dead!" rang out across America. He was the only president I had ever known.

So Harry Truman was no longer our neighbor. He had moved into the White House. Shortly after that they discovered that the White House was crumbling, so he and his family moved across the street to the Blair House while repairs were made to the White House. I have a brick from the original White House. Blair House is now beautifully decorated and is used to house visiting dignitaries.

From bustling Wall Street to Capitol Hill to the Deep South, I had the privilege of getting to know the sons and daughters of slaves and heads of state, a persecuted Jew, and several presidents. My growing-up years were unique and rich, and I am grateful for them.

CHAPTER 6

THE WAR YEARS

During the war Betty and I attended a public school, which in the beginning was frightening to me. The classes were so big and the children were so loud. The Maret School was never like this, and Ettie had always taught us to be quiet. When you live in hotels and eat in dining rooms, you have to behave yourself. We never ran in halls or yelled or carried on because that is just the way we were reared. But the children who attended public school had not been reared by Ettie!

Because I had been schooled by my father and Ettie and had attended the Maret School, I was advanced academically. As a result, they placed me ahead. At fourteen I was young to be a sophomore, and I had to compensate for inexperience. Woodrow Wilson High School was ranked the number one high school in the country at this time and was very progressive. Six languages were offered, advanced science and math, and even a mandatory sex education class (which was always packed). There were four drama clubs, which gave remarkable productions during the year. Some of my classmates became famous actors and actresses. In typing class I sat between twins whose mother wrote the bestseller, *Anna and the King of Siam*, which later became a smash Broadway hit and then a movie.

It was during my time at Wilson High that I also learned the power of the press. I joined the school paper staff and wrote a column called, "Have You Seen?" I became the gossip columnist of the school, writing items such as, "Who was the new girl with Billy J. (our top basketball player)?" and "Did you see Ellen B. and Jeanne W. at the ice skating rink with Joe and Keith?" I never reported anything negative or condemning, and I found out very quickly that people loved to see their names in print. My goal was to write about as many different people as possible. In the past the most popular were repeatedly mentioned, but I set out to change that, making the statement that everyone was important. This was fun and gave me a great deal of satisfaction.

Betty and I struggled to remain fashionable in high school. Very little was for sale during the war. Shoes were rationed to three pair a year, and a cousin with a larger foot was a treasure of hand-me-downs. My feet took the cue and stopped growing to help the situation. Because I was younger and had grown up during the Depression, all this didn't really bother me. But Betty was older and was more aware of better times. She found this period of our lives very difficult.

We both wore about the same size dress, and Ettie sewed most of our clothes. She designed and made beautiful dresses, so we always looked nice. If Betty wore a dress on Monday, I would wait and wear it to school on Thursday. Her Tuesday dress would be my Friday dress, and so on. We kept careful track with the idea of throwing off anyone who was trying to discover our scheme. Actually, no one knew that

Betty and I were sisters. She had dark hair and mine was blonde. We didn't look at all alike. We had different friends. And if we told them we were sisters, they thought we were kidding because Williams was such a common name.

Uncle Kit and Aunt Gladys, with whom I had lived as a baby, moved to Washington from Memphis. Because their daughter Julia was older than Betty and me, we began to inherit clothes and shoes from her. There was also a distant relative named Mary who sent us things she couldn't wear anymore. She sent me a red corduroy coat that I loved and wore until the material was almost see-through thin.

For my fourteenth birthday, my aunt and uncle took me alone to the beautiful Mayflower Hotel for dinner in its elegant dining room. We soon noticed that just two tables from us was Shirley Temple. Seeing her reminded me of one of my classmates at the Maret School, my friend Choo Choo, which means "little cabbage" or "precious little one" in French. When I was nine years old she moved, but she had been Shirley Temple's double in the movies. Now this famous child star was in her late teens and sitting with her mother and two gentlemen in the same restaurant as I! I thought she looked so glamorous and couldn't help but stare at her. Finally, my uncle excused himself and went over to request an autograph. He pulled out a dollar bill, which she graciously signed. This was the greatest birthday present I could have ever imagined.

I kept my Shirley Temple dollar in a secret drawer in the desk Betty and I shared. It was my prized possession, and I would take it out frequently to look at it. Betty was very aware of what it meant to me and knew where I kept it, but helped herself to it one day when her allowance ran out and she needed money. When I saw that it was gone, she said matter-of-factly, "I took it and spent it."

I was crushed. "Why did you do that?"She replied, "I needed it."

My father disciplined Betty and told her that what she had done was stealing, but she didn't seem at all sorry and my trust in my older sister was greatly shaken. As the younger sibling, I had looked up to her, and even then I didn't see that she was jealous of me. I looked like my mother, was more outgoing, and had lots of friends and dates. She was pretty in a different way, more introverted, and her dates were few. This breach of trust over the Shirley Temple dollar began a pattern of betrayal that hurt me deeply over the years, until finally and much later in life I had to accept that she would never be the sister I wanted her to be.

Because my father was a colonel in the Army, we had a few privileges during the war. The Army Post Exchange, or PX, had some meat and other luxuries that were not available to civilians. We seldom shopped at the PX, however, because it was on the other side of the Capitol and transportation was difficult. For special occasions, however, Ettie would board a bus on Connecticut Avenue, transfer to another, catch a streetcar, and arrive at the base. Whenever she did this we all felt it was worth the time and trouble.

There was little gasoline and no tires—if you had a car to drive. Although Daddy could have requisitioned extra gasoline, he would not do it. Others made fun of him for not taking advantage of his position, but he was adamant that if one person was rationed all should be rationed. He made exception to clergy and medical personnel. He said, "All else should cinch their belts."

Public transportation was used even for movie or ice skating dates, which I was beginning to enjoy. We only drove the car on special occasions, such as evening dances when we wore long, full dresses. Somehow there was plenty of gasoline for Daddy's boat, the one on which he proposed to Ettie, but we usually didn't have enough gasoline for the car to get us there. Then the Coast Guard bought the boat in late 1942. It was painted and refitted to patrol Chesapeake Bay.

Sometimes we took sandwiches to school. They were usually either peanut butter or vegetarian, as there was little meat. Our vegetarian sandwiches consisted of the beans or carrots left over from the night before and mixed with lettuce and mayonnaise. They were good, and I didn't mind—except a red beet sandwich. I took it to school but threw it away because the bread had turned red and it was embarrassing.

We lived with air raids and sirens screaming intermittently during the night and also the daytime. There were German U-boats in Chesapeake Bay at one point. When the sirens would go off at night, we'd just get up, grab our pillows, run down seven flights of stairs to an underground shelter, and stay there until it was all over. Sometimes it was a short while, sometimes it was a long time, but I never had any fear. It was just something that I accepted.

Something else I had accepted early in my life was making friends and saying goodbye to them. It was part of traveling with Daddy. But during the war and as I grew older, it became more of a challenge. One of my boyfriends during this time was named Billy, whose grandfather had piloted the famous

Graf Zeppelin. We included Billy in a boat ride one day (before Daddy sold it to the Coast Guard). Ettie always insisted that we were neatly dressed with ribbons in our hair. During the boat ride she saw that I was disheveled, hair ribbon off, and face smudged. She said, "Anne Sharp, look at you! You are a mess."

Billy immediately took up for me and said, "Anne Sharp is not messy. Anne Sharp is beautiful. She always looks pretty." Ettie was so shocked that she burst into laughter and had a hard time stopping. Shortly after that Billy's family was called away.

Even though World War II was a difficult time, I have some rich memories. We got to know some of the precious English war orphans and other young people who were deeply affected. I met one of my best friends, Alexis "Bunny" DeCastelaine, because of the war. She was from the southern part of France. Her father was Count DeCastelaine and they had lived in Monton on the French Riviera, next to Monte Carlo. He was killed by the Germans, so she and her mother, who was an American citizen, escaped to America. With a trusted servant and in a wagon, Bunny and her mother crossed Southern France and Spain and went into Portugal. Then they got passage on a freighter to New York and ended up in Washington, D.C. Bunny told me that before they left their beautiful home on the Mediterranean, her mother gathered all of her jewelry and anything valuable that they could carry to finance their escape. I never forgot that.

CHAPTER 7

UNSEEN HAND

Ettie had experienced the trauma of war as a young child, and she was very fearful during these years. She had just married my father, had no idea where her family was in France, and was extremely frightened of losing my father to the war. Although he never saw combat in World War II, we had no idea where he was or what he was doing when he was gone. And, as it turned out, his involvement in the war cost him his health and eventually his life.

No matter what I faced as a young girl, however, I always had a sense that someone was looking out for me, particularly when it came to my safety. When I was three, I had fallen from the main entrance landing of a brownstone boarding house down to the stone steps below, crushing my head. I regained consciousness and remember Daddy blowing the horn of the car, racing through traffic, and Ettie holding me on her lap.

When we arrived at the hospital, I felt no pain. There was a lot of yelling and rushing around. People kept saying, "She's losing blood," and something about pressure increasing. The last thing I remember seeing was Ettie's white dress drenched in blood. I didn't realize the blood was mine. Then someone said, "She can't see."

I know now that it was no coincidence that one of the leading surgeons in the country was in the city to do a seminar that week. Dr. Shagrue performed a remarkable new operation to relieve the pressure on my brain and remove pieces of my skull. There was no permanent damage or paralysis and I regained my sight. The only thing that worried my father and Ettie as I recovered was how to tell me that my head was completely bandaged. They were concerned about how I would react when I saw myself for the first time.

They decided to send in a very creative doctor. He held a large hand mirror behind his back and had a white cap covering his hair. He said, "Well, I see you have a white hat on your head too. I think my hat is prettier than yours, though. Would you like to see yours so we can compare?"

After a little teasing he held the mirror in front of my face. I announced, "Mine's the prettiest because I'm a girl!" There were no worries after that!

On another occasion we were on my father's yacht on the Potomac River and a violent storm hit. It was evening and the sky became pitch-black. Everyone put on life jackets, and I sat below on a top bunk with Betty and our cousin Julia. My father was at the wheel trying to get us back to port, but turned it over to another adult to check on us. He came down the steps and asked me, "Are you afraid, Anne Sharp?"

"No Daddy. I'm not afraid." Somehow I knew that we would all be safe. When this story was told when I was older, I learned that seventeen vessels capsized that night and many lives were lost. Some of the boats that were lost were larger than ours and some were smaller. Historically this is known as one of the most violent storms that area has ever seen.

One of Ettie's favorite stories also took place in Washington, D.C. I was five years old, and we were living in a boarding house. Being close to Christmas, the place was quite festive with its Christmas tree in the hall. The cars at that time had running boards on the sides to help passengers step into them. This was especially convenient for our dog, whom we named "BA," which was short for Betty Anne). She would hop on the running board of our green Chrysler when we took her along and sit there until we stopped. Then she would hop off and follow us as we walked.

Three days before Christmas Eve, we all decided to venture downtown. It was snowing, BA jumped onto the running board, and off we went. We did not realize that when we stopped at a red light, BA jumped off the running board, thinking we had reached our destination. When we finally stopped and got out of the car, we discovered she was gone.

This was particularly heartbreaking because I had recently been hit by a drunk driver and had a cast on my arm. (I had a string of accidents as a child.) Although I had been sleeping in a regular bed by this time, I now had to sleep in a crib so I wouldn't fall out and injure myself more. The crib had two missing bars at one end, and when I was awake I could get in and out through that hole. Needless to say, my life was a challenge and BA was my sympathetic companion.

Daddy put an ad in the lost-and-found section of the *Washington Post*, and every night we prayed for God to bring BA home to us. On Christmas Eve, he heard me plead, "God, bless Daddy and Ettie and Betty and all the boarders, but most of all you know I need BA. Please bless BA and bring her back to me."

In the background the boarders downstairs were chatting. Daddy and Ettie were trying to prepare me that I might not see BA again when the voices became louder and more excited. There was a commotion on the stairs and then scratching at our door. Daddy opened it and in flew the dirtiest, hungriest dog you ever saw. BA jumped through the hole in the crib and into my arms. I cried, "See Daddy, I knew God would hear me! May BA sleep with me tonight?"

Ettie fed BA and no one seemed to mind a little girl sleeping in a crib with a dirty dog. We never found out how BA found her way back to us in the snow, but the boarders, Ettie, and my father knew that God had answered a little girl's prayers.

CHAPTER 8

FINDING MY WAY

At the end of the war my father came home very ill. Today we know that this was due to radiation exposure from the atomic bomb test, but back then nobody knew (or no one was saying) why he was so sick. He suffered from internal bleeding and was at Walter Reed hospital a great deal. When he was discharged he was still so weak that he couldn't read, so I enjoyed reading to him.

In the spring of 1946 I graduated from Woodrow Wilson High School in Washington, D.C. That summer I turned seventeen and enrolled at Mary Washington College in Fredericksburg, Virginia. My sister and I entered a beauty contest, which was more of a bathing suit competition, and the freshman class sponsored me. She won second place and I won third. This is one of the bright moments in what was a very difficult time because of my father's illness.

Betty and I often dated cadets attending the Naval Academy at Annapolis, and that was where I met Don. He was about six foot four and very handsome—and strong. He actually saved my life once. During his senior year at Annapolis I went up for the weekend. We went out on a picnic and crossed to the other side of the river. On our way back, we decided to cross over the river on some railroad tracks. Suddenly we felt the tracks vibrating and then we saw a train coming. Without hesitation Don quickly swang down under the tracks, holding on to the timbers with one arm and leg, and pulled me down beside him, holding me in his right hand.

I was literally dangling over the water! When the train had passed, he simply pulled me up until I could grab the railroad ties, and then he boosted me over. He climbed up after me, and neither one of us said a thing through this whole episode! For such a big man, he struck me as being very gentle and caring, and I felt very secure with him. After he graduated he was immediately shipped out, but we corresponded.

I managed to finish a year and two quarters at Mary Washington College, which was part of the University of Virginia, when my money ran out. You are probably wondering how the granddaughter of Senator John Sharp Williams and the daughter of Allison Williams could be in such dire straits, so I will explain. Although my father had been extremely wealthy in stocks and property before the stock market crash of 1929, the crash had wiped out his assets, and during the Depression he found himself cash-poor. He still owned several businesses and all of the homes he had built or purchased in Mississippi and Tennessee, but they brought in little income during the Depression. His commission into the army during the war brought some steady income, but not enough to put me through an expensive college.

It wasn't until several years after the war that my father's financial situation rallied. The US economy began to boom, the businesses he owned began to produce considerable income, his real estate holdings became valuable, and his knack for investing wisely in the stock market began to pay off again. However, during and for several years after the war we lived very frugally. Now I had to find a school with affordable tuition.

During that summer of 1947, Betty married a graduate of the Naval Academy. My father was in the hospital and could not attend the wedding, so my uncle, Admiral Joel W. Bunkley, gave her away. He was the admiral in charge of running New York City Harbor. I was the maid-of-honor, and although it was my sister's big day, I was so concerned about my father that I had to fight back tears the whole time.

Since my father had always been a registered voter in Mississippi, I applied to and was accepted by the University of Mississippi, or Ole Miss as it is called. I got a ride to Oxford, Mississippi, with some people from Philadelphia, Pennsylvania, whose son was also enrolled. I arrived with $111.00 in my pocket and was immediately recruited for sorority rush.

Since there had been no sororities at the University of Virginia, this was all new to me. The girls in the dorm told me I needed a black dress, and I managed to find one for $11.00 at Neilson's, near the courthouse. I enjoyed the whole process of rush and in the end, with some pressure from one of my roommates, pledged Chi Omega. I met many wonderful friends as a member of that sorority. Forty years later, some of these same sorority sisters would come to my aid in a great way.

I needed to find a job, but my faculty advisor said, "It is unthinkable that the granddaughter of Senator John Sharp

Williams would work. No. Not at Ole Miss." I was shocked at this attitude because I had gratefully worked when I was at Virginia. Now I had $100 left and $50 went to registration. Since I didn't have money for books, I bought paper and pencils and started attending classes. Now I felt alone and far from home, especially since my father was so ill and my sister was married. I drank Cokes for breakfast and luckily had dates for lunch and dinner. The boys were fascinated because I was a "Southern Yankee" and used a cigarette holder.

The short time I was at Ole Miss was loads of fun even though I was way out of my league as far as my age was concerned. After all, I was eighteen years old and because of my academic record, I was placed as a junior. Nearly everyone was a year or two older than I. The students and faculty were wonderful to me, however. Our servicemen were returning from war "older and wiser" and wanting to get their education, so the campus was flooded with eligible men with money from the GI Bill. They were full of ambition, and marrying a "Southern belle" was icing on the cake to them. Everyone wanted to be lighthearted, have fun, and forget about the war.

I easily fell into the festivities. My picture was on the cover of the campus magazine, and I was often on the front page of the newspaper. Ole Miss was making the most of having the granddaughter of Senator Williams attend their school. But I continued to struggle with money. When my Uncle Kit and Aunt Gladys (who had moved back to Memphis) invited me to stay with them for a while, I was rescued from a very stressful situation. The Dean of Women at Ole Miss wrote several times to try to get me to return, but I had to decline. They just couldn't fathom the fact that I needed to work. I attended Ole Miss from September to December of 1947.

There was another important reason I had decided college was not for me. The choice of professions for women was limited to teacher, secretary, or nurse; and none of those interested me. I wanted to be a lawyer or engineer, and both of these fields were closed to women.

Now in Memphis, I met all the "right people" and worked as a model in department stores and dress shops. Because my feet were especially small, I was also in great demand at shoe stores. When a shoe representative arrived in town, I was called to display his line of the latest styles. My aunt bought me some nice clothes and I attended all the social functions. I also attended a quiet little Episcopal Church with her. I felt comfortable on my knees at St. Johns.

Sometime during my stay in Memphis, I realized for the first time in a long while that I felt safe. With my sister married and living across the country, my father so ill and Ettie consumed with caring for him, the lack of money, and all the friends who had come and gone during the war, I found myself in a loving family who genuinely cared for me. Up until this time, I really had no idea how the war and the fragmentation of my family had affected me so deeply. However, all this time I had been corresponding with Don regularly and things had become more serious.

After being with my aunt and uncle for several months, Don wrote from Japan and asked me to marry him. I replied and told him that I couldn't give him an answer to his proposal at that time. When he got back to the States shortly after that, he called and asked me to meet him in San Diego. My sister and her husband were stationed there, so I flew out and stayed with them. About ten days after I arrived, Don received orders to ship out again. We said goodbye, and he gave me some beautiful stones he had purchased overseas for my engagement ring. He told me to have them set while he was gone. I said, "I'll wait."

It was during this time that my brother-in-law's commanding officer took me out occasionally. He was a lieutenant commander from Texas named Jack. He began to see me more frequently and said that he had called his mother to fly in and meet me (he was an only son). He was serious, but I wasn't because he was much older and I really thought I was going to marry Don. His mother turned out to be one of the loveliest ladies I had ever met. I even stayed with her at her penthouse suite in the hotel. After her visit Jack kept insisting we should get married, but I was rescued when my brother-in-law was reassigned to the East Coast and I needed to accompany my now pregnant sister on the train to their new home in Lakehurst, New Jersey.

That summer a friend from my old childhood camp called and asked me to come and be her junior counselor. Not knowing what else to do, I accepted her offer and spent the summer near Port Jervis, New York. After camp, I returned to Lakehurst, and my sister had her baby on August 25. My joy over the arrival of my niece was cut short the day my brother-in-law informed me that Don had been killed in a plane crash.

Nineteen years old and numb, I went to Philadelphia for a visit with my friend from the summer camp. That is where I met Dick. He was thirty-two years old and asked me to marry him within two days of our meeting. In my confused state, I said yes, but in the following months and in the excitement of announcing our engagement and planning the wedding, I grew to love and trust him. Two weeks before we were to be married, however, he said, "I probably should have told you this before, but I am adopted." I was completely taken aback by the fact that he hadn't trusted me with this information earlier.

I said to him, "What else have you hidden from me?" and we proceeded to have an argument. The issue was never his adoption but his lack of trust in me. In the end, I didn't feel secure and called off the wedding. I put an announcement in the various newspapers that "by mutual consent" the marriage had been called off. This was March 1949 and I was almost twenty years old. I was living in Washington, D.C., to be near my father and look for some kind of work. I immediately found a job in a bank as secretary to the vice president, but I certainly was not a secretary. I just sat in the middle of the lobby at a great big desk, my name in gold letters on a mahogany stand, and greeted people as they entered. This was right up my alley and I loved it! I was more of a social director than a secretary. I worked there for a little over a year and my life seemed to settle down some.

During this time Jack contacted me. He was stationed on the East Coast, around Newport, and we began talking and seeing each other occasionally. He told me that he had received permission from the Cardinal to marry me outside the Catholic Church, but our children would have to be raised in the Catholic faith. I told him he was wonderful, but I just did not love him that way. I learned later that when he got out of the service, he returned to Texas to run the family oil holdings.

In the spring of 1950 I left my job to travel to Europe with two friends of mine. In London I was honored to receive an invitation from Ambassador Lewis W. Douglas to the royal parties at Buckingham Palace, and I met the Queen at her annual Garden Party. In Paris, I was invited to the embassy parties by Ambassador David Bruce. In Germany, I was graciously received by the American Counsul General Sam E. Woods at the embassy and as his personal guest at his castle outside Munich. Mr. Woods was married to one of the Anheuser-Busch daughters, and they had completely refurbished the place.

In Rome I met my uncle, Admiral Bunkley, and he took me to some beautiful places and great parties, with people like Rita Hayworth and her fiancé Prince Aly Kahn, along with Barbara Stanwick and her husband Robert Taylor. Movie stars and Hollywood moguls were everywhere. By sharp contrast, Senator John C. Stennis arranged for me to see the Pope. There were thirty of us that went in at one time. I also went to Switzerland, Monte Carlo, and other wonderful places.

When I returned in September 1950, I applied for a job with the Bureau of Standards. As standard procedure, the government had the FBI check me out, and it took them several months to trace all the places I had lived. There were approximately thirty-three addresses. When my application and clearance were approved, I got the job and enjoyed it immensely. I felt they paid me very well for doing very little.

My father was feeling better, so he and Ettie went down to visit his brother John at Cedar Grove Plantation. While he was there the Mississippi Congressional Society honored me by asking if I would enter the Miss Cherry Blossom Festival contest, representing Mississippi. This is a very large annual affair in Washington, D.C., commemorating Tokyo, Japan's 1912 gift of three thousand cherry trees to the United States. The trees were planted around Washington's Tidal Basin, and the yearly flowering of the trees is exquisite.

I entered the contest as Miss Mississippi and, as it turned out, I won. It was a wonderful experience. I met girls from all over the country, and the Eisenhowers treated us like royalty at the White House. We were paraded down Constitution Avenue, were given all kinds of gifts, and were sent escorts every evening for personal appearances. One of my escorts was a good-looking naval officer from Mississippi with whom I became reacquainted when I lived in Jackson years later.

Not long after the Cherry Blossom Festival, my father, who was still at Cedar Grove Plantation, began bleeding internally again and was taken to the hospital in Vicksburg. I wanted to go see him, but Ettie and the doctors told me not to come then. Finally, he became so ill that she called and said, "The doctors say to come if you're going to see your Father before he dies." I caught the train to Vicksburg and had no idea that my life would never be the same again.

CHAPTER 9

DECEPTION BEGINS

I was the only person to get off the train at the little story-book station in Vicksburg, Mississippi. The stationmaster peered at me through his glasses behind the barred window. I asked, "Would you mind calling a cab for me, and could I get a red-cap for my bags?"

Now he really stared at me. Presently he said in a Southern drawl, "Where to? We don't have red-caps."

"I'll be staying at the Vicksburg Hotel," I said.

"That's just over the viaduct," he informed me.

I pressed, "I really do need a cab. I have several bags."

"Okay Miss, " he replied, so pleasantly. I thought he would make a good ambassador for the people of Vicksburg.

He called for a cab, and I told the driver where I was staying. After checking into the hotel, I called Daddy's hospital room. Ettie told me to come on, so I went immediately. When I first saw my father my heart sank. He had had frequent blood transfusions and was unable to sit up. He looked so pale that it astonished me. I couldn't imagine not having him in my life. I was tremendously grateful that Ettie was there to care for him and share my grief. He was so precious to both of us that we clung to each other.

Ettie was frightened. She was in a strange part of the country in an old hospital that had been used during the Civil War. She couldn't get the nurses to help her care for him, and by the time I arrived she was exhausted. We spent a lot of time talking, and it was during this time that she told me about Mrs. Flowers.

My father's oldest sister was married to Judge Edwin R. Holmes, who was the Chief Justice of the Tenth Circuit Court in New Orleans. Her best friend had a younger sister named Hester Flowers, who lived in Vicksburg. Mrs. Flowers brought flowers (and this is no joke!) every week to my father's hospital room. One day Ettie mentioned to her that I would be coming down to see my father.

Hester Flowers was born Hester Craig, and the Craig's were very well known in Mississippi. When my grandfather, Senator John Sharp Williams lived in Yazoo City, his family always sat across from the Craig family in the Presbyterian Church. Mr. Craig was a successful cotton broker whose two older sons became even more wealthy due to cotton and sugar brokerage contracts. At one time one son had a seat on the New York Stock Exchange.

This Yankee family of Irish descent arrived after the Civil War and had money to invest in a defeated South. They were well-liked, but it was not until John F. Kennedy was elected president of the United States that they openly declared that they were Irish. They had always claimed they were Scottish because the Irish were greatly despised for many years in the

South. Too many had flooded in during the 1850s.

The Craig's financial success had carried them into high Southern society, and now Ettie informed me that we would be having supper with one of them, Mrs. Flowers. The chauffeur picked us up at the hotel and drove us to the Flowers' home. The house was immense, but the exterior struck me as odd. The British architecture had been compromised by adding Southern porches and verandas. People referred to this as "bastard English."

This home had been built by W. C. Craig, Mrs. Flowers' father, who had come to Vicksburg and purchased the Newit Vick property on Cherry Street. Newit Vick was one of the founders of Vicksburg. The Craigs tore down the Vick home and completed this huge structure in 1902. It is the largest home in the area to this day.

The front yard was lovely and long, with a brick-enclosed, elaborately designed rose garden to the left. The three-story home had a full basement and wine cellar, as well as a carriage house and large stable in the rear. Each suite of rooms had walk-in closets containing combination safes for valuables and jewelry, and the bathrooms were tiled and ornate.

The house had been wired for electricity and plumbed for gas just in case electricity didn't turn out to be such a good idea. The coats of arms of the Craig family, Ireland, and Scotland were set in stained-glass windows on the second floor landing of the main staircase. As we entered the main foyer, light shining through the glass was simply magnificent. To the right was a large parlor that was also used for dances. The furniture was Louis the XV and XVI, and it seemed shocking to go from a heavy, dark, oak hall to a light, airy French parlor and ballroom.

What was originally the dining room was like a baronial hall with a fireplace made of stone. The mantel was so tall that I could easily stand under it. After her husband died, Mrs. Flowers converted the room to a living room, and this is where she received Ettie and me. She greeted us warmly. I liked her immediately and it was reciprocated. She said, "I've seen your pictures in the newspapers recently" (because I represented Mississippi in the Cherry Blossom Festival). "You are as lovely as your pictures."

The housekeeper served drinks before dinner, which was very shocking to me. My father had given up drinking when he became a single father, and we never served alcohol in our home. Although I was familiar with social drinking since I dated older men primarily, drinking in a family setting was new to me. We moved to a screened-in porch near the rose garden and visited beneath a slowly moving fan.

Mrs. Flowers informed us that she had two married daughters, one in Boston and the other living on a plantation south of Vicksburg. She said, "My only son lives here with me. He's a lawyer, a deacon in the church, and still not married." Then she laughed and added, "I don't believe he'll ever get married. Goodness knows, the girls have tried, but he keeps escaping. I've told him he's going to get too old, and he'll be sorry."

After a pleasant evening and as we said our goodbyes she invited us to church on Sunday. Ettie declined, of course, but I accepted gladly. The next day she called to say that her chauffeur would pick me up at 10:45 a.m. Sunday morning. That morning I put on a square-necked, pink, silk shantung dress and a medium-brimmed hat, which framed my shoulder-length blonde hair. In those days there was no question of telling boys from girls. Women wore hats, white gloves, and beautiful dresses. Also, by the way, thank-you notes were promptly written, handkerchiefs carried, etiquette most important, and polite manners unquestioned. Therefore, I was downstairs a little before 10:45 a.m., ready when the car arrived.

Mrs. Flowers and I got along famously, and I thought she was absolutely delightful. We had traveled to the same places, knew the same people, had seen the same plays, and had read the same books. We had even been to Queen Elizabeth's private garden party at the same time the previous year. She showed me the newspaper clipping of me as Miss Mississippi in the Cherry Blossom Festival, which she had cut out and saved. She had other clippings of me from other Eastern papers. I didn't think anything of this and was highly complimented by her attentions.

As we sat down in her customary pew in the Presbyterian Church, she said, "Save a seat. My son is going to join us." I slid over in the pew closer to her, and the service began. The next thing I knew, I looked up and saw this tall, good-looking man walk through one of the doors at the front of the church. He wore a white linen suit, had blonde, curly hair, and was very muscular. He had arrived late, but just in time to do his deaconly duty of passing the collection plate. Suddenly he slipped into the seat next to me.

Since the service was in progress, Mrs. Flowers introduced her son Grey to me in a hushed voice. Our eyes met and it seemed like sparks of electricity flew everywhere. Soon he turned and said, "I hope you don't think I'm being fresh, but do you mind if I place my arm behind you on the back of the pew?" Then, as an afterthought, "It's a little warm in here without air conditioning." The fans were slowly rotating from the ceiling above.

I smiled and answered, "Not at all," but I thought it an unusual request.

We shared a hymnal and I noticed he had a beautiful, strong singing voice. I wondered if he would be joining his mother and me for Sunday dinner. My question was answered when the service was over and he said to his mother, "I'll take Anne to pick up a paper and get some ice cream for our dessert. We'll meet you back at the house." He took charge immediately.

As we left the church he boldly slipped his arm around my waist. I liked how he guided me to his car, but I was unnerved by his familiar manner. He was relaxed yet calculating, chivalrous yet moving in quickly. His car was a beautiful, black, Buick convertible with red leather seats. The top was down and it was parked under a large oak tree. He opened my door and I got in. He spoke easily and assuredly to me. We arrived at the drug store, and he helped me out of the car. As we entered, I heard a long, low whistle. It was a friend of Grey's. After seating me he walked over to his friend and I heard him say quietly, "Don't even look at her. She's mine."

We had a Coke and talked for a short while, got the ice cream, and drove to the Flowers' home. I was introduced to the housekeeper, his mother joined us, and the three of us had a delightful Sunday dinner together. Grey always played golf on Sunday at one o'clock, but that day he canceled and took me to his plantation. We had a wonderful afternoon. Ceres Plantation was located eighteen miles from Vicksburg on a winding gravel road near the Big Black River. At that time it consisted of 463 acres and there were several buildings on it: the Flowers' home (built around 1845), several barns, and a charming lodge that Grey had converted from a sharecropper's cabin. This was his bachelor's quarters, complete with stone fireplace, music, and mood lighting.

Later that evening Grey took me to dinner at a very nice Italian restaurant in Vicksburg. We drove around the city and the park for a while and then he took me back to my hotel. He kissed me goodnight, and I was completely swept off my feet. The next morning he telephoned from his office and asked if I would join him for breakfast at the coffee shop. I said, "Certainly."

I went downstairs, and we had coffee and a little breakfast. Then he said, "I want to take you to see my sister's plantation." Being an impressionable young woman, I now believed everybody had a plantation in Mississippi. All the ones I knew did!

We went to his sister's place south of Vicksburg, which was called Broadacres. On the way back, at twelve o'clock noon, he pulled over on the gravel road and asked me to marry him. I said yes without hesitation. He was handsome. He was nine years older than I was. He was established. He was a lawyer. He was a deacon in the church.

I trusted him.

CHAPTER 10

A FORBIDDEN KISS
AND HONEYMOON BLISS

"I'll go see the Colonel tomorrow and ask him for permission to marry you," Grey said excitedly.

"But Grey, he's too sick. This will be such a shock. It might hurt him," I countered.

"We'll go back to the hotel and I'll talk to your stepmother first. We'll ask her what to do," he said. "After that, I'll have Mother invite you over for dinner and then we'll tell her."

"Not me!" I said. "I'm not saying anything. You'll have to tell her."

We met on Sunday, he proposed on Monday, that evening we told Ettie, and on Tuesday he went to ask my father's permission to marry me. Ettie prepared my father well for Grey's first and most important visit with him. And it didn't hurt that Grey, who was the same blood type as my father, had given blood for his next transfusion that morning. That morning my father had also consulted with the Presbyterian minister to make certain Grey Flowers was a man he could trust. After receiving a favorable report and seeing how much Grey loved me when he met with him on Tuesday afternoon, he gave his consent.

On Wednesday we dined with Mrs. Flowers. I was so excited that I couldn't eat anything, but I remember how beautifully her maid served the meal. Afterward Grey and I sat holding hands on a love seat, and Grey told her he was going to marry me. She was thrilled and immediately plunged into planning the wedding. This was fine with me because Ettie was consumed with caring for my father. It seemed natural that she should step in to help.

As a wedding gift, Mrs. Flowers wanted to send us to South America on a two-month honeymoon, but Grey thought that would look bad for a lawyer who was trying to build up his business. Some time after we were married I mentioned the offer to my mother-in-law and she said, "My dear. You'll learn that opportunity seldom knocks twice at the same door." I never forgot that lesson!

The story of when Grey and I met was one that he loved to tell. He especially loved the fact that we had fallen in love at first sight. On Saturday I caught the train to Washington, DC, to pack all my worldly possessions, resign my job, and move to Vicksburg to be married. He wrote wonderful love letters to me during the five or six weeks I was gone. He flew to Memphis and had a beautiful marquise diamond he had bought years before for whomever he would marry set in platinum and baguettes.

Fortunately for me, his older sister came down from Boston to take charge of the wedding with her mother because I had no idea what to do and did not return to

Vicksburg until four days before the wedding. While I was in Washington they made all the arrangements, reserving the Presbyterian Church for the ceremony and the country club for the reception. They used my pictures from the Cherry Blossom Festival for the newspaper announcement of the engagement. They ordered, addressed, and sent all the invitations, but they did ask me whom I would like to invite. They even picked out our china, silver, and crystal.

When I finally returned from Washington, I did not realize I was about to go through a tremendous culture shock, from living in the big city to living in a small town; but I was too blinded by love to understand what I was doing. In fact, I was so blind that I had forgotten what my husband-to-be looked like! I arrived at the Vicksburg Hotel early and prayed he wouldn't be in the lobby. I hurried to get my key, caught the elevator, and ran to my room. Pretty soon the telephone rang and it was Grey. He was downstairs and said, "I'm here. Come on down."

I said, "Oh no. You come on up." I wasn't sure I would recognize him and was afraid I would jump into the arms of the wrong person! Soon there was a knock on the door. When I opened it I knew him immediately and wondered how I could ever have forgotten.

It was three days before the wedding, just in time to attend a few parties. My sister had sent her wedding dress from Norfolk, Virginia, to Mrs. Flowers' home. It was there when I arrived. She came to town just in time to be my matron-of-honor, wearing a dress of her choice. All gifts were sent to the Flowers' home, and Mrs. Flowers and

Grey's sister opened and catalogued them.

At the wedding rehearsal the Presbyterian minister who would perform the ceremony informed us that no one would be kissing in the church. He said that he had not kissed his wife until their wedding reception, and I immediately felt very sorry for him. So we were resigned that there would be no "you may now kiss the bride" from him at the conclusion of our ceremony.

The wedding took place August 3, 1951. It was an evening affair at Vicksburg's First Presbyterian Church, and the reception was held at the Vicksburg Country Club. A complete floor-and-a-half at the hotel was reserved for out-of-town guests, and despite the short notice people came from many parts of the country to attend. However, my father missed his second daughter's wedding even though he was in town.

My Uncle, Judge Edwin R. Holmes, gave me away. As I walked down the aisle I was extremely happy, but when I looked across the crowd I noticed many people were weeping, and that surprised me. At that moment I deeply felt the absence of my father. The rest of the ceremony was a blur except for one thing. Before Grey and I started up the aisle, my new husband grabbed me and planted a kiss that lasted so long the congregation began giggling and murmuring. When we finally came out of the embrace, my glance fell upon Mrs. Flowers, who—to my relief—was laughing uncontrollably. Grey and I walked out of the church without a backward glance at the minister.

We went immediately to see my father in the hospital. I was in my wedding dress with my new husband, and the first person I wanted to see was Daddy. He was so sick, I wondered if

I would ever see him again. As we got off the elevator on Daddy's floor, patients and staff were lining the hallway. Someone had told them we were coming. They clapped and cheered as the bride and groom made their way down the hall. During our visit I was very quiet, which is unusual for me, but Grey was enthusiastically going on and on about how much he loved me and how happy he was. He made this very difficult time much easier for me. We did not stay long and then left for the country club.

At the reception there were two bowls of punch. One was called Presbyterian punch and the other was heavily laced with alcohol. Because Mississippi was a dry state, all liquor was bootlegged. Nearly everyone from Vicksburg attended the laced punch bowl. Unfortunately, the photographer my sister-in-law had chosen (who was later a Pulitzer Prize winner) went to the wrong punch bowl. Since the minister did not allow any pictures to be taken at the church, there weren't but three pictures taken at the reception, and they were cockeyed. And so I do not have a photographic record of my wedding except for a few snapshots friends took.

After the reception we went to Mrs. Flowers' home to change. My new husband's two sisters and a cousin got into a big argument while I was dressing to leave. The cousin had had too much to drink and went after one of the sisters. I was in shock to see two women fight physically, and then relieved when the other sister broke it up.

I dressed as quickly as I could and went out to the upstairs hall. When I was on the third landing of the grand staircase I saw Grey on the second landing with his arms outstretched. I literally jumped the steps into his arms—and he caught me!

My feet never touched the staircase.

We drove to Jackson, Mississippi, for the first night, and checked into the honeymoon suite of the Heidelburg Hotel under an assumed name. I will never forget when we got off the elevator and followed the bellman to the room. Above the door was a blue neon sign that said, "Bridal Suite." I said, "Oh no! I don't believe that sign!" But when Grey picked me up and carried me over the threshold, I had no more thought of it.

The next day we went to the Grand Hotel in Point Clear, Alabama, where we spent the rest of our honeymoon. We had a glorious time getting to know each other, planning our life together, dancing near the water's edge, and walking barefoot on the beach. Grey bought little gifts for me every day and flowers arrived often. We swam and sailed and never wanted to leave. I think the staff began to wonder if we ever would. One morning at breakfast Grey was looking into my eyes dreamily and poured the cream into the sugar bowl, then stirred his coffee. It was something this smooth-talking lawyer would never live down. The staff reminded us of this incident for years to come whenever we stayed there.

Suffice it to say, our honeymoon was a tremendous success and neither one of us wanted it to end. Our physical passion for each other was always the central part of our relationship and held the marriage together for as long as it lasted. In that arena we were extremely well-matched. It was such a wonderful beginning.

CHAPTER 11

ELLA

Grey and I were married only weeks after we had met, and anyone with any sense could tell that I didn't really know him. Despite the incredible physical attraction and delirium of love, I was more of a trophy than a partner to him, and he was not someone with whom I felt comfortable sharing my innermost thoughts. I tried in the beginning, but he just didn't seem interested. As a result, I soon stopped opening up my heart to him. I compartmentalized my marriage: sex in the bedroom, hostess in the living room, mother to the children, and social activities in the community.

Shortly after we returned from our honeymoon, he took me out to Ceres Plantation again. I mention this because something very interesting occurred. That day I met Ernest Flowers. Actually, I first noticed the big plantation house east of Ceres, which is where Ernest lived. It was in fairly good condition and quite impressive. The top was down on our convertible, so as we approached Grey slowed the car to avoid stopping in a red dust cloud. He said, "There's somebody I want you to meet over there."

Ernest was standing by the gate to his property and I was struck by his appearance. He looked like Grey, with the same blue eyes, facial features, and wavy hair. There was one major difference, however. He was a very light-skinned black gentleman, and I emphasize "gentleman." His hair was white, as he was much older than Grey, probably about the age Grey's father would have been had he lived, and his manner was extremely genteel.

Grey said, "Ernest, I want you to meet my wife."

Ernest smiled and said politely, "Well, I'm glad to meet the missus. I thought it was about time you got married." He looked closely at me. "You done well."

Grey asked about his crops and how he was doing, and then we drove on. I waited to ask Grey about this very distinguished and well-spoken man. He said, "Ernest is my father's first cousin. During the Civil War my grandfather's brother left the country and went to Europe. When he returned he moved into the plantation house over there and lived with a former slave woman, who bore him two sons, Earnest and his brother. I don't know where the brother is. When the old man died, he left the property to his two sons." Grey paused and then said that they "lived quietly." He didn't seem at all embarrassed about Ernest, but I asked no more questions. I was aware of the law prohibiting marriage between whites and blacks.

As Grey Flowers' new bride, many people were very generous to me. I met a nice man who gave me a piece of property in a beautiful subdivision of Vicksburg. He just gave it to me! Grey could not get a loan without his mother co-signing, and he was ashamed to even ask her. So we built our first home on the property with the stocks and bonds I had brought to the marriage. The deed to the property was put in his name so that his credit rating would improve. I thought nothing of this.

Our social life was full, and I was very happy about that. One thing Grey appreciated about me was that I am a complete sanguine. I am extremely outgoing and have a great memory for names because people are very important to me. When we were at parties, Grey would stand beside me while I made contacts for him. He was also pleased that I enjoyed entertaining and did it very well. However, because I had grown up traveling and Ettie didn't cook very much, I had no knowledge of the kitchen. His mother and sisters gave me cookbooks, but after Grey lost thirty pounds in the first two months we were married Mrs. Flowers hired a cook for us.

Soon I was pregnant, and Grey was ecstatic. So was I—even being sick as a dog the entire pregnancy. When our oldest son arrived, you would have thought a royal prince had been born. The entire Flowers family and the surrounding community went crazy and showered the baby with gifts. I wrote 110 thank-you notes. Grey, on the other hand, showered me with gifts. Being the only male in the Flowers family, he was extremely grateful that the first child I had borne him was a boy. However, he made it clear to me that the children were going to be my responsibility. He would hire any help I needed to do the job, but his involvement would be limited.

Grey's words shocked and disappointed me, as I had enjoyed such a close relationship with my own father and wanted that for my children. The truth was that Grey had very few memories of his own parents. He had been reared by servants and sent off to boarding school when he was young. The family life that I loved so dearly was a complete mystery to him.

When the baby was about six months old, Grey gave me another surprise. One day he said, "I just can't sleep with anyone," and exchanged our double bed for twin beds. This was very upsetting to me because I missed being close to him and it made me feel like a kept woman.

Grey's law practice had never taken off, so he took a job as an attorney for the makers of Pine Sol and Gala Bleach in Jackson. Our move on New Year's Eve 1952 was a memorable event for me. Grey had gone on ahead with the movers, and I was coming later with Ettie, her maid, and the baby. We had a blowout on the way, and a passerby stopped to put on the spare tire for us. Further down the road, we had another blowout. With no more spare tires, I nursed the baby, handed him to the maid, then hitched a ride back to Bolton. Since it was New Year's Eve, I asked the driver to take me to the city jail, as I knew it would be open and safe. There I called my father, who was sick in bed. He arranged for a man from a tire company to drive to Bolton, pick me up, and take me back to our car, where he changed the tire and sent us on our way again. We arrived in Jackson three to four hours late. Grey had been worried and was glad to see us.

Unfortunately, Grey's job did not last long. He got into a fight with his boss and was fired. I called a friend of mine from my Washington days, who offered Grey a job in the insurance business. About that time, my friend's mother passed away and his father moved. Their housekeeper was out of work, so I asked her to come to work for me. This turned out to be one of the best decisions of my life.

Ella and I partnered in "family business" for nearly thirty years. At this writing she and I have been close friends for over fifty years and still talk every week or so. She was with us during the years we were in Jackson, which were our best family years. We lived in four different homes there. My favorite and the one we lived in the longest was the third home on St. Andrew's Drive at the Jackson Country Club. The house was around seven thousand square feet and backed up to the golf course. It was so large that one day a truck pulled up to deliver meat, thinking our house *was* the Country Club!

Ella was hired as a domestic servant, but she never really worked for me. We had too much fun! We worked and played together, and Grey paid her. We liked each other from the moment we met. I was chauffeur, grocery shopper, and children's play organizer. Ella made the house and the children shine, and her wisdom and sense of humor helped to set a wonderful tone in our home. Also, I was the envy of the community because she was extremely skilled in everything she did.

We entertained so much that Ella kept a record of our guest lists, particularly what was served to whom on what date. That way we were sure not to serve our friends the same dishes over and over. Whenever a party was planned, she and I would discuss the logistics, make decisions together, and then carry out the plan. And we had a tremendous time doing it!

The main thing Ella and I shared was a love of children and family fun. People would shake their heads at me and say, "How do you stand it? If I had all those children, carting them around in that station wagon day after day—and their friends most of the time too—I'd go crazy!" Honestly, I never really thought about it as a task. It was simply a wonderful life. We would sing, run spelling words, talk about what was going on at school and with friends. I loved every minute of it.

We were forever trying to plan family outings that would include Grey, but they were few and far between because he didn't like to travel with children. I wanted our children to experience the "family picnic," like I had enjoyed when I was a child, and I finally convinced Grey to go with us. He said that if we were all going to do this, then we were going to do it right. This meant buying "equipment" for what turned out to be a one-time event.

We left right after church on Sunday with Ella and four children, setting out to find the perfect spot. We drove and drove and finally found a place near Port Gibson complete with lake, ducks, and picnic tables. Ella had prepared a delicious rib roast, salad, corn, rolls, and dessert. We had brought a tablecloth, silver goblets, silverware, cloth napkins—and even wine. But by the time we reached our destination, the children were starving and just wanted to eat with their fingers. They certainly did not want to set a nice table and be civilized! In the end, it was quite an occasion that Grey did not want repeated.

I must explain that we were not "putting on the dog" here. People in Grey's social circle could not fathom eating on paper plates, using plastic utensils, drinking from a paper cup, or even using a paper napkin. It simply was not done. Using anything but sterling silver, china, and good linens was unthinkable. Ella was perfect because she understood this.

One beautiful Saturday in the fall, Grey was out at Ceres Plantation and I got the bright idea of taking the children out to meet him. "We'll just go out and pick pecans and let the children play," I said to Ella. She agreed that it was a good idea, so we packed up diapers, bottles, Cokes, food, plus baseball bat and ball. Everyone piled into the station wagon and we took off.

When we reached the plantation, the first thing the children spotted was a big tire swing. It was a huge tractor tire hung from a large tree limb by a thick rope. Immediately the voices rang out, "I want to swing! I get to go first! No, me first!" In a large family you learn to stake your claim right away.

Grey came out to greet us, heard the "discussion" and said, "I'll try it first to be sure it's safe."

Ella and I exchanged a glance and she quickly said, "Mr. Flowers, that's strong enough for these small children."

But Grey missed her hint and insisted, "Well, I need to be sure."

At this time our heaviest child was under eighty pounds; while Grey was well over two hundred pounds. Ella and I looked at each other, then watched as Grey climbed into the tire and began to swing back and forth. Back and forth and back and forth while the children were all crying, "My turn! My turn!"

Then suddenly the rope broke and down fell an astonished Grey, tire and all. Ella grabbed the smallest child and ran to the other side of the big tree. Her hand was clamped over her mouth to keep from laughing out loud. There he was, breathless and sprawled on the ground with a tire around his middle, and Ella peeking around the tree with her face all contorted. I couldn't control myself and laughed out loud. It was not a pretty sight. The children never got to swing, and Grey was furious and wouldn't speak to me for days. Yet another outing had turned out to be not what I had hoped.

Ella made such a difference in any disappointment or difficulty. She saw the humor in every situation, which helped me to keep going. But she also enriched our lives with her own life experiences and personality. She taught the children how to fast-dance. At times they went to her with their problems, as she was a great listener. And we all knew that Ella's real passion was professional golf. She knew everything there was to know about the golf pros (Arnold Palmer and Jack Nicklaus were her favorites) and would watch our boys play the "blue nine" behind our home. Among other presents, we always gave her a subscription to *Golf Digest* for Christmas.

Ella and I went through heartache and triumph together, and she loved and cared for our children like her own. I remember when Robert, our youngest son, was in kindergarten. She had always dressed him for school, but one morning she sat down beside him on his bed and said, "Now, you're getting to be a big boy. You're going to have to start dressing yourself. So this will be the last day that I will dress you." Robert had tears in his eyes, but the next morning he came downstairs fully dressed with a smile on his face. When she told me about this, I laughed because it was like she had weaned him. I think the measure of the part Ella played in our lives was that Robert was a good-sized boy before he realized that her last name wasn't Flowers!

CHAPTER 12

ALL MY CHILDREN

To understand the level of devastation I experienced later in my life, you must first understand how important my children were to me. Although my life was compartmentalized, they were the most important part and I loved them dearly. Grey was our first-born. He was such a beautiful baby and a handsome boy. My father called him, "My little partner," and their love was mutual. When my father died, it was a severe blow to Grey.

Grey was a quiet child because, unbeknownst to us, he could not hear or see very well. When he was in first grade, we had him tested because his speech was not clear and he couldn't see the blackboard very well. The doctor operated on him and he regained almost one hundred percent of his hearing. We also got him glasses, and he was delighted.

Despite these problems early in life, however, Grey always made friends easily, and they were loyal to him. Although he was always sought after by the girls, at this writing he has never married, but professionally he has been quite successful in the area of finance.

Our next child was a beautiful, auburn-haired baby girl. The entire family was ecstatic over her red hair because no one had ever had it before. Julia turned into a beautiful, somewhat shy, bright young lady. She tended to be a loner. The rest of us would be outside playing but she preferred to stay in her room. So I encouraged her to participate in after-school activities. Because she was so gorgeous, the boys were generally intimidated by her, but after getting two degrees in college, she married a doctor and had three sons.

I miscarried my third pregnancy in the third month. Then my fourth pregnancy and our third living child was another son, who was strong, active, outgoing and very blonde. Ella's sister came to see him and commented, "I declare, that is the whitest white child I ever done seen!" Craig was highly motivated and had a habit of doing all his homework before going out to play. I got up early during the week to drive him to school because he was a patrol boy, then went home to get the rest of the children and take them to school. Today he is a doctor, is married, and has three children.

There is always a plan in each person's life. It was the seventh year of our marriage and I was twenty-seven years old when I discovered that I was pregnant for the fifth time. This was not planned, and I was distressed. When our first child was born and Grey had told me he didn't want to be the kind of father I had assumed he would want to be, I still hoped. I thought that being around his children would change him. However, by this fifth pregnancy I realized that he was never going to change, and I was angry because I felt like a single parent. Ella was a great help, but the weight of the task was mine and I was tired.

Some of my friends had had abortions because they just couldn't handle any more children, and they encouraged me to do the same. I made an appointment with my doctor and explained my plight to him. He looked at me intently, then gently said, "No, that is something I cannot do." In those days, no one really thought of an early pregnancy as anything but a blob of flesh—certainly not a living human being. Therefore, my doctor was sending the clear message that what was inside me was alive. I understand how shaky and desperate women can feel about an unwanted pregnancy, but I am eternally grateful to my doctor for saving me from the heartache of abortion.

Later I realized my ignorance had nearly caused disaster because this baby turned out to be our fourth living child, my darling Elizabeth. She was sweet, calm, cuddly, and about the nicest baby you could imagine. She fit in well, gave no trouble, and was easily loved. As soon as she could walk, she was outside playing with her brothers and their friends. They loved her and called her, "Be Be," which is French for "baby." As Elizabeth grew older she made friends easily. She grew into a beautiful girl with big blue eyes, thick blonde hair, and a ready smile. Elizabeth earned two degrees in college, traveled a great deal, and married a minister. They have eight children!

My next pregnancy did not go full term and was stillborn. Because I now had a firm understanding that a pregnancy was a baby from the git-go, I had picked out names and this was devastating. I felt the grief of losing a child. It wasn't long before I was pregnant again, however. Our fifth living child was a very big boy and another delight. Al and I were close, and when he was little he always wanted to sleep in our room. He too was very handsome and also athletic. At eight years old he won the children's city golf championship and later won the Gilette Hole-in-One competition, receiving $50,000. He was very adventurous, loved playing football and rugby, and entered college only to drop out after a year.

Al took a job on a Mississippi tugboat, and on the docks of New Orleans was known as "Big Al" because of his enormous strength. He met his wife in a bar and they eloped. Then he went into the military and became a ranger, paratrooper, and expert marksman. He was highly favored by the officers because of his good manners and ability to play golf. After leaving the Army, with two children, he returned to college and earned a degree in business. He's a hard worker and a fantastic husband and father, and he and his wife have five children.

Our sixth living child was our youngest son, Robert, who is described in more detail later in this book. And our seventh child and youngest daughter was Debbie, to whom I dedicate a full chapter.

Having babies and rearing children was the center of my world and the delight of my life. They were on my mind from the time I awoke until I went to sleep at night, and I was involved in their lives as much as a mother can be. This was such a special time in my life, such wonderful days.

CHAPTER 13

IN SICKNESS AND IN HEALTH

I was having the time of my life being Mrs. Grey Flowers of Jackson, Mississippi, and raising our children with Ella. Although Grey's lack of involvement with the children was disappointing, he and I had many times when we truly enjoyed one another, especially when he took me on extended vacations. Our relationship worked when he was wining and dining me away from the children. So we traveled often, and he took me to many wonderful places all over the world.

From the beginning of our marriage he had stated, "I will never go anywhere unless it is first class." His practice was to arrive at some exclusive hotel and tip everyone lavishly "to insure proper service." The doorman, bell captain, bellboy, hall maids, and every waitress or waiter were well paid.

We went to major resorts in the US, to Europe, and to many exotic islands. There was one spectacular private island in Venice, Italy, complete with a launch and two-man crew. Ciprianni was one of our favorite spots, where each luxurious night costs $700.00 (this was a lot in the 1960s). Then there was the hijacking adventure. We were on our way back from

London on a chartered plane, which was supposed to be on a direct course to Jackson, Mississippi. However, we noticed that the plane was flying very low and didn't seem to be headed in that direction.

The whole affair was very calm, and I believe it was because the plane was full of lawyers. The hijackers picked the wrong plane because some of the lawyers simply talked them out of it! We landed in Bangor, Maine, where they were removed from the plane, and then we proceeded on to Jackson. I remember that while we were in the air, before the hijackers had been persuaded to give themselves up, the drinks were flowing more freely than usual. Other than that, it was a very pleasant flight.

With all this travel, we were happy that Daddy had rallied after our marriage and his health was improved, so he and Ettie would stay with the children. Ella was there as well. Once in a while my father would comment that he wondered where Grey got the money to live the way we did, especially when he didn't seem to work that many hours. Grey's professional life seemed to be a struggle for him from the beginning. I came to believe that he really didn't know how to relate to people unless he was drinking and partying, especially after the job that had brought us to Jackson didn't last but five months. Afterward he took the job as an insurance salesman, but he had what is called "call reluctance." He couldn't handle rejection in any form, so he suffered there for years, killing his pain with alcohol.

After we were married Grey carried on his family tradition of having cocktails before dinner every evening. By the time we were living in the large country club house, the cocktail hour had increased, and he often went without dinner. It got to the point where I didn't know if the drinking was causing his problems or his problems were causing him to drink. But one thing was certain. He was miserable. He had become very much a loner with few friends, rarely played golf anymore, and didn't know how to really enjoy his family. The only social interaction he had besides spending time with me was when we were at a party or having a party.

Our evening routine was well established. Grey would come home from the office, and I would have the children fed, bathed, ready for bed, and lined up for him. He would kiss them goodnight, and the maid or Ella would take them to bed. Grey and I would go into the library, where I would have an assortment of hors d'oeuvres ready. Broiled oysters wrapped in bacon, toast points with caviar, oysters poulette, and cheese straws were some of his favorites.

Grey had had a series of deadbolts installed on the top of the double doors to the library, which he would lock as soon as we entered. Then he would fix us drinks, we would share the hors d'oeuvres, and he would tell me about his day. Eventually, as the drink began to relax him, he would begin to tell me of his plans for his life. Every night he wanted me all to himself with absolutely no interruptions. Hence, the deadbolts.

I didn't realize it until I was older, but my outgoing, upbeat nature was a terrible irritant to Grey. I managed to stay that way even though I had one child after another and was pregnant nine times in fifteen years. Losing two babies was extremely painful, but I threw myself into caring for Grey and the children to get through the grief and go on. I bounced back and he became somewhat jealous of my happiness with family and friends.

Locked in the library each evening, after he told me about his day, he would ask me to tell him every detail of my day. As a newlywed, I was extremely complimented that he was so interested in me. As the years went by and the drinking increased, however, the nightly accounting became more unnerving. I began to wonder if he trusted me. He seemed to look for any discrepancy in my story, often making comments that implied I was carrying on with another man or spending money in ways I shouldn't. Still, life was a bearable and a basically pleasant routine until 1959, when everything changed drastically.

We had had four children, and I had just gotten out of the hospital after giving birth to the stillborn baby and having surgery as a result. It was a difficult time in my life, but I had little time to grieve. There was an epidemic of viral encephalitis in different parts of the country. Twenty-one people in Mississippi were infected, eighteen in Jackson, and Grey was one of them. In the end, he was one of the two who survived. The other was a young boy who became a vegetable and died in an institution later, when he was in his thirties.

When encephalitis struck Grey, I sent our children away to stay with relatives and tried to nurse him back to health at home. He was too sick to move. He moaned and cried out. It seemed that he was in terrible pain, and I felt helpless. I sat beside his bed continually, sleeping in a chair because we had twin beds. My hands were often red and swollen from the ice-cold cloths I was applying to his feverish head. He was unconscious most of the time. If I bumped the bed, he would cry out in pain.

The doctor came by several times a day, but nobody knew

much about encephalitis or what to do about it. I asked questions, but neither he nor anyone else I contacted had any answers. We did not know that it permanently damaged the brain. One thing became clear as the death toll mounted: people simply did not come out of a severe case unscathed, and most didn't come out at all.

Grey was never himself again. After he "recovered," he continually suffered head pain. The doctor tried various drugs, but nothing seemed to help, so his drinking began to escalate even more. He couldn't work for well over a year. When he did begin going to his office, he had trouble making decisions. His reasoning ability was impaired, he didn't know what was happening most of the time, and he had severe mood swings. He was full of unexplained anger, and one day he got into a physical fight with his boss.

I took him out of town for a while, hoping that he would become more relaxed and balanced. I also took him to other doctors, hoping they could find a physical answer for him. Maybe there was a drug or a treatment. All of these attempts proved fruitless. Eventually the reality set in that he was never going to be the same. This was a terrible blow, but I determined to find a way to live with him the way he was—violent, paranoid, and sick physically.

I noticed there were a couple of things that made Grey more peaceful and less angry. I have said before that we were well matched in the sexual arena, and that continued. Whenever we made love, and sometimes if I just sat with him and stroked his hair, he relaxed and became quiet. To be honest, I began to use sex and physical affection to keep him calm. It gave him hours of peace afterward, but it was more

107

than that. It was the only way we could experience each other like we had before he became ill. On some level it soothed my soul as well.

And so we had three more children after Grey's bout with encephalitis! One of those children was our youngest son, Robert, whose arrival was a bright spot in our troubled lives. Grey loved to tell the tale of Robert's birth. We had rushed to the hospital as we always had in the past, the doctors and nurses began to attend to me, but this time Grey stayed with me instead of going to the waiting room or going out to do something else. The doctor announced, "It will be awhile. I'm going downstairs to grab a bite."

The nurses disappeared, and Grey and I were alone in my room. After a few minutes, the labor pains increased dramatically, and since I was well familiar with the process, I knew I was a lot closer than the doctor had thought. "Get the doctor, Grey, quick!" I hollered. He immediately rose to run out for help when I cried, "No! Don't leave me! Help me!"

Grey simply took hold of my bed and began wheeling me into the hall. He was extremely excited and began yelling, "Nurse! Nurse! I need help! She's having the baby!"

By now I was pushing and the baby's head was crowning. Thus, Robert Clark Flowers was born in the hall at St. Dominic Hospital, his father attending as the nurses rushed to our aid.

"Look Grey, he's here!" I exclaimed, looking down at the end of the bed.

"Don't touch him," he said. He seemed frightened.

I laughed, "Why not? He's mine." But before I could pick

him up, the nurses began wheeling me into the delivery room, and Grey stayed right outside the door. The doctor arrived shortly and picked up the baby, who started crying. They let me hold him before putting him in the incubator because he was so cold.

Grey called this the second highlight of his life, the first being our falling in love at first sight. I wanted to call the baby Robert, but Grey insisted we call him Clark. When he graduated from high school, however, our son chose to be called Robert, which is why I refer to him as Robert in this book. Grey favored him from the moment he was born and took a special interest in him. Robert's birth was one of the rare sweet moments we shared after Grey had been struck with encephalitis.

I also noticed that having parties made Grey feel better. Being around people took his mind off his problems. I had always given great parties, but now I gave them even more. Wonderful cocktail parties. Fancy dinner parties. Party, party, party to try to make things better. My life had become a whirlwind of activity that now included being a caregiver.

As early as our honeymoon, I had noticed that Grey was somewhat of a hypochondriac. He had brought what I thought was a golf shoe bag. I asked him if he was going to play golf and unzipped the bag to take out his shoes. To my surprise, the bag was filled with bottles of pills. We laughed about it at the time, but after the encephalitis the hypochondria became extreme. I was constantly taking him to various doctors or the emergency room, especially for feared heart problems. These symptoms were usually proven false, but then he also developed diabetes. Now I was doing my best to see that he ate correctly, as well as taking care of the children.

With all these responsibilities and more babies, I was thankful I had Ella's help. This allowed me to continue to do a great job of hiding Grey's problems from the children and all of our friends and family. I became a wonderful enabler. When Grey couldn't go to the office, I would call them and say, "I'm so sorry, but Grey's got a sinus headache, and he won't be in today." A few days later I would call again and say, "Grey has to get the car fixed. He'll be in later." Then I would call later that day and say, "Grey wanted me to call and let you know he's got an appointment and he'll be in tomorrow."

I thought I was protecting the family by maintaining our income and benefits. So I lied and lied. That was also part of the culture of the South, especially in the social class in which we circulated. It simply was not acceptable to have the kinds of problems we were having.

The encephalitis not only left Grey very angry but his jealousy turned into a rage. He was now convinced that I was being seduced by other men everywhere I went, so he sought to control my entire life. The nightly report in the library became an interrogation. He demanded to know the friends I had seen, activities I had taken part in, how much I had spent—down to how much gas I had put in the car.

He would give me a certain amount of cash every week and I would account for every penny of it daily. If I shopped at a store and didn't have enough cash, he had told the stores to call him to get approval for my purchases on his account. A few friends, Ettie, and my sister were aware of this and thought it ridiculous, but I told them that it was not a good idea to defy Grey in any way. His anger was explosive and now sometimes violent, and I wanted to avoid it at all costs.

Grey had a tight grip on all areas of my life. As I look back, it is amazing that I managed to continue some outside social activities. In Jackson, I was a member of various organizations. I was listed in 1965 as one of the Who's Who Outstanding Young Women of America because of charitable work. I was named the Outstanding Junior Member of the Daughters of the American Revolution for two consecutive years and later Outstanding Member for the entire state. I was an officer in The Colonial Dames of America, Chapter XV, a small but exceptionally interesting group of women.

As a member of the Junior League, I was asked to organize the old Capitol Guides in Jackson. The next year I had thirty-two members, and shortly after that we started a state docent program to train the volunteers. At the time I was in charge it was the largest volunteer program in the Junior League. One of my favorite projects in the League was driving for the Florence Critenton Home for Unwed Mothers. It was a great place for someone like me, who was always pregnant or carrying a baby on her hip. The troubled girls felt at ease with someone who was usually in the same condition.

One year, when I was about six months pregnant, I was to pick up six of these pregnant girls and take them for a fun afternoon at the Mississippi Arts Festival. Some of my children had put gum wrappers in the ashtrays of the car, and when one of the girls started smoking, we soon found ourselves choking on fumes. I immediately put on the flashers, honked the horn, and flew down the road to the nearest gas station.

The station wagon swerved into the gas station, smoke

coming out of the windows and horn blasting. We came to an abrupt stop, all doors flew open (including the rear), and out jumped seven very pregnant women, coughing and tears running down their cheeks. Eyes wide, the gas station attendant rushed over and cried, "What's going on?" in a high, falsetto voice.

"We're on fire," I said calmly. This really scared him.

"My God! You're next to my pump!" he hollered. "We'll all blow up!"

"Oh, just get that little water squirter you've got for radiators and squirt some in the ash tray on the back seat door. We'll be okay," I assured him. He stared for a second and then did as I asked. In the meantime, two other attendants had run out to help. The looks on their faces were comical. I don't know what shocked them more: the sight of so many pregnant women or the smoke coming from my car. After the fire was out and the smoke cleared, we all hopped back into the car, thanked the men for their help, and proceeded toward the Arts Festival, where we had a marvelous time.

With a friend I also established the first blind Brownie Troop in the state. I loved these children. Each week I picked them up in my convertible and took them to my home. They loved that car! They touched the top, and as I opened it up they could feel the wind and sunshine on their faces. I was able to obtain money for uniforms for all of them. These were bright moments in an otherwise dark time.

CHAPTER 14

TURNING POINTS

In 1966 my beloved father finally succumbed to the ravages of radiation poisoning. He and Ettie were living in Vicksburg at the time. I had spent as much time as possible with him through the years, making certain my children knew him. They adored him and it was reciprocal. He was a very loving, stabilizing influence in their lives. At the end, I was at the hospital every day, driving in from Jackson. Then one day he stopped breathing. The doctors were able to bring him back, but our next visit proved to be something I never anticipated.

I walked into his room, took his hand, and he said, "Let me go, Baby. I've only been staying here because of you." His eyes were shining and his face aglow. "I've already been there—I saw Papa and Mama, I saw Grandpa and Grandma, I saw John and Webb and Sharp—please let me go." He paused, and then he said, "Now, I know you are going to be all right. Please Baby, let me go back."

I was so shocked and upset that I pulled my hand from his, turned away, and walked around to the foot of his bed.

Grasping the iron frame, I mustered all the strength I had and gasped, "I'm letting you go." Then I began crying so hard that I said, "Daddy, I have to go home now." I kissed him goodbye and left the room.

The phone rang at three the next morning and the doctor told me that Daddy had died. He was buried at Cedar Grove Plantation among six generations of family. I knew that my protector was gone, and for the first time in my life I felt very much at the mercy of my circumstances. My inheritance from my father, which was considerable, was handled by Grey. He and my sister's husband, now a Chancery Judge in Vicksburg, were made co-trustees of our father's trust and the inheritance, which went to Ettie, my sister Betty, and myself. When my checks arrived, they were in my name and Grey would have me endorse them. Then he would deposit them in his account. I knew nothing of our finances. Later I discovered that my money had contributed over $600,000 to what Grey called "the pot," and that other stocks and bonds that were part of my inheritance were cashed to buy our large house near the country club in Jackson.

Just a year after Daddy died, in 1967, I was diagnosed with cancer of the cervix. When I told Grey, he asked, "What are you going to do about it?"

Our seventh living child, Debbie, was just a few months old. I said, "I'm going to continue nursing the baby as long as I can."

The doctors kept a close eye on me, and five weeks later it was apparent that the cancer was growing rapidly. I needed an operation right away and was to go immediately to Oschner Cancer Clinic in New Orleans to have a hysterectomy. The day I left, I gathered all the children together and told them that they would be fine while I was away. Ettie and Ella would take care of them. I told them that I was going to the hospital for an operation and would be okay, but it might be awhile before I got back.

Just then my sister Betty and brother-in-law arrived and insisted on taking the baby to their home. I cried and begged them not to, but they said that Ettie and Ella couldn't handle all of the children and a baby by themselves. I told them I wanted my children to be together. Betty ignored me and went upstairs, gathered together some clothing and diapers, and got Debbie out of her crib. There was no more discussion. Grey drove the car up, and as we drove away from our home at the Country Club I was very uneasy.

Although Grey went with me, he took this opportunity to party while in New Orleans. He had two aunts, many cousins, and a number of old acquaintances there. Some days he would come to see me, and other days he would not. He had an accident in our new car while he was drinking, but he wasn't injured. However, the police found a gun in the glove compartment and arrested him. He called one of his aunts, who bailed him out of jail. He then went to the Cadillac dealer and purchased another brand-new car.

That night I received a surprise visit from Grey and the man who had sold him the car. I was dismayed that he would bring this stranger to see me because I was so ill. The next day he arrived at 11:30 a.m. He said he was going back to Jackson and would make arrangements to get me in a couple of weeks. I felt totally deserted and angry. Once again he broke his promise to stand by me. When he made a promise to me, it was hard to remember that he was very ill and would most likely forget the promise or not be able to keep it. I was continually hurt by this.

As soon as Grey left I telephoned Ettie in Vicksburg and asked her to come. She said she would. However, Grey called her a few minutes after I did and told her not to go because he was taking care of me. She had always been afraid of Grey and was too intimidated to oppose him now. She called to let me know what he had said. When I tried to call her back a little later, Grey had had my hospital phone disconnected. He had, however, prepaid a private nurse to be with me at all times because the doctor had ordered this. I was now isolated.

Three weeks later, when it was time for me to leave the hospital, Grey did not return to get me. The doctor had an ambulance take me to the airport, the attendants put me on a plane for Vicksburg, and a friend of mine met the plane with a wheelchair. My friend took me to Ettie's home, where Ettie nursed me for the next five weeks.

Ettie drove me home, and when I arrived Grey took one look at me and said, "You'd better get in bed." Then he told me that he wanted me to give a Christmas party for his office staff the following weekend. The older children were in school, and Betty still had Debbie, but the younger ones and I had a great reunion. When the older children returned from school they all sat on my bed and we caught up on everything they had been doing. It was a joy to be home with them again.

A week later Betty brought Debbie home because I still couldn't drive. When I took her in my arms, she seemed so changed, and not just physically. She was not the warm, cuddly baby she had been before. After that, whenever I held her and loved her, I felt such resistance. Even now it is painful for me to remember, knowing what this meant in years to come. I didn't really have time to brood about the lack of affection in my baby girl, however, as I was busy planning the Christmas party and getting back into the routine of taking care of Grey and the children.

To deal with the difficulties of life with Grey, I planned summer "escapes" for the children and me. Because Grey was so jealous, Ettie would go with us as chaperone for me! Grey was sure men were trying to lure me into hotel rooms while I was away. I would try to reason with him, "Grey, I've always got children in tow. Believe me, no man is interested in seducing a a woman with seven little children around her." He remained unconvinced, so I was glad Ettie was there to be a witness of my good conduct. And because she was hard-of-hearing, all the chatter and noise of travel and being with children didn't bother her. Julia, my oldest daughter, brought earplugs!

One summer we would go west and the next summer we would go east. Several years we went to different areas in Florida. The two older boys would pack and unpack the car, putting most of our luggage, including a stroller, on the top of the station wagon. Exciting things happened on these trips, and we had a tremendous time. Robert took his first steps in Dallas, Texas, and Debbie learned to walk in Sarasota, Florida.

Whenever we were about to check out of a motel, they always wanted "one last swim." Because I was so easygoing, I never had a problem saying yes to things like this. But what do you do with seven wet bathing suits on a road trip? We would catch them in the rolled-up windows and let them dry in the wind as we traveled down the road. We were a sight to behold!

My children were each assigned jobs according to their age and abilities, and they were nearly always very well behaved. One time we joined some friends in the Tennessee Mountains. They had only one child, and when we pulled up they were in shock at the sight of us. My friend told me later, "I didn't know whether to laugh or go into hiding!" They were pleasantly surprised at the good manners of my children. Ettie would always tell her friends, "Anne has the loveliest, most beautifully behaved children. They are a joy to go with on vacation."

Like my father, I stopped whenever there was an historical site, museum, art gallery, or anything in God's creation that interested us. Ettie taught the children French songs, which they mostly didn't understand, and there were many humorous incidents. At an art gallery one day, Ettie had Robert by the hand, and he was just beginning to talk. They stood before a "Madonna and Child," and Robert began chattering away and pointing to the nakedness of the baby Jesus. Ettie never did understand what he was saying, but my daughter Elizabeth and I hid behind two marble columns and giggled. We waited until Ettie took Robert on his way, complimenting him on his enthusiasm for the work of art.

CHAPTER 15

THE CLUB

Throughout my life, there has been one thing I simply cannot tolerate, and that is injustice. Many people have read John Grisham's novels or have seen the movies made from his novels, which tell stories of corruption and injustice in the South. Mr. Grisham knew what he was writing about because he lived in Mississippi and graduated from law school at Ole Miss. He also served a term in the State House of Representatives. Mississippi has had one of the most corrupt legal communities and unjust judicial systems in the United States.

One of my favorite examples of this has to do with the fact that the state was dry, and many people bought alcoholic beverages from a man named Red. A bootlegger who lived across the Pearl River, Red supplied all the august members of various communities with illegal whiskey. He delivered to our house in Jackson and to the plantation on many occasions. Red was a very wealthy and powerful man.

One day Red was tried and found guilty of murder. The papers, however, reported many testimonies from outstanding citizens. They attested to Red's good character and generosity to orphans and the Baptist Church. When it was time for the judge to pass sentence, he asked Red to stand and said, "Red, we know you're a good man. You've done so much good in the community and in the church. I know you mean well, so I'm just going to put you on probation."

Had Red been poor, black, and without knowledge of illegal transactions with nearly every major official and leading citizen in the state, he would have received an entirely different sentence. More than that, if the judicial system in Mississippi was run by law and not good-ol'-boy connections, the victim and the victim's family would have received justice. Instead, Red went back to bootlegging and his prices went up.

Until my personal, head-on collision with judicial corruption, I was vaguely aware of it being close to home. Not only was Grey a very wealthy and socially connected attorney, but you will remember that my sister Betty married a naval officer, who later entered the legal profession. They were living in Norfolk, Virginia, when Grey and I were married. Shortly after my marriage, Betty's husband, Lieutenant, Jg, Nat Bullard, decided to leave the Navy and attend law school at Ole Miss in Oxford. They had little money and two children, but the GI Bill, Betty's ingenuity, and a little help from my father saw them through.

Because Nat Bullard was a Yankee, when he graduated from law school, he had a difficult time finding a position with a Mississippi law firm. Grey and Daddy helped him search, and eventually Bullard was introduced to another lawyer named John Pruitt. Bullard was offered a position and a chance to buy into his firm in Vicksburg, so my father put up $10,000 to buy a job in the firm for him. Betty and their children moved to Vicksburg to begin a new life. This was especially nice because Daddy and Ettie were also living there.

Times began to improve for all of us. It was the mid-fifties. Pruitt's and Bullard's law firm added Gerald Braddock and then Travis Vance. They built a new building and prospered for many years until one day it all crashed down around them. My brother-in-law told us that there was a misappropriation of firm funds to pay one of the partner's gambling debts. And then there was the little matter of Travis Vance's death.

Vance had disappeared and his boat had been found overturned in the middle of a river. His body was never recovered, he was presumed drowned, and declared legally dead so the insurance money would be delivered to his heirs. However, the life insurance company became suspicious when a claim was filed on the Vance Estate. They began an investigation and located Vance, who was very much alive in Texas. He was disbarred and sent to prison for fraud and falsifying his own death. Not too long after, he was "miraculously" set free. And on top of all that, he was reinstated to the Bar Association of Mississippi and resumed his law practice in Vicksburg! He later hired Bullard's son, first as a clerk when the boy was in law school and then as a full-time attorney. At this writing Vance still practices law.

After the misappropriation of funds and Travis Vance's scandal, Braddock and Pruitt moved into another building to start another law firm, and Bullard decided to run for mayor of Vicksburg. He won and served one term, giving all the city's legal work to Pruitt and Braddock. After one term of being mayor, he joined their firm, which eventually became Bullard, Braddock, Gee & Gee (Pruitt left). The two Gees were Bullard's daughter and son-in-law, who also had attended Ole Miss Law School. The son-in-law was well liked, and the law practice flourished. The Gees bought a big, new home.

The Bullards and Gees were very active in the Presbyterian Church in Vicksburg, and many clients came from there. They became officers in the church and taught Sunday school. When we moved to Jackson, we began attending the Presbyterian Church there. Grey and many of his cohorts were deacons and elders in that august body of "believers," and they continued to be listed as such whether they were serving prison time, had divorced their wives and left them penniless, or were engaged in criminal or immoral acts. A favorite joke in the community when McCarthy was scouring the American countryside for communists was this: Are you or have you ever been a member of the Communist Party or the Presbyterian Church? Even Grey would say this and laugh. Unfortunately, this bastion of hypocrisy and deception was where my children were raised and most continued to attend after they were adults.

Eventually some of Bobby Gee's clients became suspicious of his actions. This prompted an investigation, which uncovered the fact that Gee had forged Chancery Judge Thames' signature on many types of legal instruments, filing them as completed and then collecting a sizeable fee. He was prosecuted and found guilty of forgery. It was an uproar that was quickly and quietly slipped under the judicial rug. He was merely disbarred and told to leave Vicksburg. Gee went to boot camp and became an officer in the army. He served in a high-ranking position in the US Army Military Police

Corps. He never spent a day in prison and is now retired as a full colonel.

Around the time of covering up why the Gees left Bullard's law firm, Judge Thames died and there was a vacancy in the Chancery Court. I would discover the extensive power of a chancery judge in the years to come. My brother-in-law, Nat Bullard, began a vigorous campaign to obtain the judgeship. Through financial and social influence he won and was sworn in as Chancery Judge of the Ninth District of Mississippi. One of the attorneys whose practice grew considerably while he practiced in Judge Bullard's court was the same Travis Vance. It is also interesting to note that when Judge Bullard died, Gerald Braddock was Chancery Judge, keeping the judgeship under the control of the same group of attorneys to this day.

Judge Bullard and Grey Flowers were co-trustees of the A. R. Williams Trust, which was intended for Ettie, my sister, and myself. All of the men in the legal community that I have named, as well as many others, were financially and socially connected to my husband and this group.

One of the organizations that enabled Grey and his friends to pull all the strings in business, law, and politics was the Capital Investors Club. This club was founded by my husband and others when they were starting out as professionals. Its purpose was to share information about investments, and this exchange paid off. Over the years they prospered and their parties and group vacations became more lavish.

Many politicians, including governors and senators of the state, became members of this prestigious club, which included bankers, doctors, and lawyers. One of the bankers served time in federal prison after being convicted for fraud. In fact, several members served time over the years. Another trend I began to notice as the years went by was that many of these men were either divorcing their wives and marrying younger women or carrying on a series of affairs, even bringing their mistresses to club functions.

Most of the couples in the club drank heavily, but this was the norm for all of our social circles. I recall one particular party when Governor and Mrs. William Winter, who were members, were there. The conversation was even more crude and rowdy than usual, which was very embarrassing to some of the women. I never attended again and neither did Elise Winter. Grey would go without me. When I spoke with some of the other wives, many said they hated the club but were afraid not to go because they might lose their husbands.

The club began innocently enough but became a means of making the members the power brokers of the state. They were intimately connected in real estate, oil, banking, politics, and legal matters, which was good and bad. The good was that many improvements were made and bills passed speedily without contending with a lot of red tape. The bad was that a lot of fraud, corruption, and collusion were accomplished and covered up. Innocent parties were destroyed if they got in the way of the "good-ol'-boy" system, which always protected their own. I was about to discover this first-hand.

CHAPTER 16

THE LIGHT GOES ON
AND THE BATTLE COMMENCES

In 1979 Grey decided that the solution to all his problems would be to sell our beautiful, country club home in Jackson and move to Ceres Plantation. No one was happy about this, but in those days the husband decided these things without input from any family members. What was most heartbreaking was that Ella would not be with us anymore because she lived in Jackson and had no intention of moving to the country.

Ceres Plantation had been leased for the previous ten years to U.S. Senator James O. Eastland. I had known him since I was a girl, in Washington, just before the war. Back then, Mississippi Senator Pat Harrison had died before his term expired, and Governor Paul Johnson had sent a delegation to Washington to ask Daddy to take the appointment, finish out the term, and run in the next election. Daddy was honored but decided the political arena would not be good for his family, so he declined. The Governor assured him he would have no trouble being elected. When Daddy still refused, the Governor tried to appoint his good friend Woods Eastland.

Woods also declined but suggested his son, James, who was appointed. This was Senator James O. Eastland, who by 1979 had served for nearly thirty years.

During his stay at Ceres Plantation, Senator Eastland made many improvements, the most notable being that he managed to have a private telephone line installed from Ceres to Jackson, and the phone company treated it as a local call instead of long distance. Because he entertained many dignitaries there, he kept it nice. Interstate 20, which runs across the entire state of Mississippi, also runs right through Ceres, which contained the only privately owned cloverleaf and overpass on the interstate. The interchange was named and is still called "Flowers Interchange." Ceres was a noticeable showplace seen from the road, complete with a huge sign that said, "Ceres Plantation, established 1820, owner—Grey Flowers."

Grey sold our lovely country club home, and we housed our large family in several condominiums in Jackson until the home on the plantation had been sufficiently remodeled to accommodate us. Grey was a perfectionist and often repeated, "Everything should have a place, and everything should be in its place." Anything he did had to be just right. And the new and improved Ceres Plantation was no exception.

Grey not only spent a good deal of money remodeling the plantation home, but he also borrowed heavily to buy the equipment necessary to turn the plantation into a working farm. Finally all the work was completed to his satisfaction, and in May 1980 our family made the big move.

As lovely as it was, living at the plantation was terrible. We were isolated. There were no neighbors nearby. We were out in the country and I loved the city. My children were lonely and missed their friends and school in Jackson. I was completely miserable as well. But God was behind the whole thing. He had decided that it was time I met the one whose unseen hand had protected me and kept me all these years.

After six months of living in the wilderness I heard about a Bible study that everybody in Jackson was attending, so I decided to join the group. I wasn't seeking God. I just wanted to be with people! This was an interdenominational Bible study at the Galloway Memorial Methodist Church, and they were studying the Old Testament book of Isaiah.

I had no idea what or who Isaiah was, but I was finally meeting some people and having adult conversation. They had already finished chapter forty when I joined. When we got to chapter forty-three and I read the first verses; however, the lights came on full blast inside me. It was like the Father was whispering to me, "Fear not: for I have redeemed thee, I have called thee by thy name; thou art mine. When thou passest through the waters, I will be with thee; and through the rivers, they shall not overflow thee: when thou walkest through the fire, thou shalt not be burned; neither shall the flame kindle upon thee."

For the first time in my life I realized I belonged to God. He had named me. He was part of my life and had been all these years. I was so excited. Jesus had become real to me. He died on that cross for me. He redeemed me. He was resurrected to give me a new life. When I was born again, I didn't just give my life to Him; I jumped into His arms! I couldn't get enough of Him, and I clung to Him. My Bible came alive, every word deeply touching my heart. All I wanted was to know more and more about Him.

During this amazing time, I started having trouble sleeping because of severe pain. The doctor thought I had arthritis and put me on some pain medication. One day I picked up the Sunday newspaper and read an article about a doctor in New Orleans who had discovered a way to diagnose fibromyalgia and treat it. Sensing this was really my problem, I made an appointment with him. He not only diagnosed fibromyalgia but found a stomach ulcer. I had no signs of arthritis, and evidently the medication I had been taking for it had given me the ulcer.

The treatment required me to stop drinking alcohol, coffee, carbonated drinks, and tea. And I have to say that this is probably what saved me from becoming an alcoholic along with my husband. When your life is that miserable, it is easy to want to drown yourself in a bottle, especially if it makes your husband happy, and I was well on my way.

All these factors made things worse with Grey, who was more depressed than ever because of our financial situation. Turning the plantation into a working farm had proven disastrous, and so our evening "meetings" in the library turned even bleaker. He was enraged that I was attending a Bible study and threw a fit every time I read my Bible or any Christian book. I'd go into the bedroom to pray or to read, and he'd come in and yell at me. He was even more angry that I was no longer his drinking buddy. He raged and ranted, but I stayed sober and continued reading my Bible.

Our Presbyterian minister's wife led the Bible study I was involved with at the Methodist Church, so I went to her for advice. Even though doctors had told Grey to stop drinking, he was insisting that I buy alcohol for him. She told me that I should obey my husband. God would honor my obedience. So I continued to buy the alcohol.

One night something particularly unusual happened. Grey was watching television and drinking while I was reading. He stood up to get another drink and, with the oddest look on his face, said, "I don't see how you do it. I have to admire you. I don't believe I could do without a drink." Up until that moment, it had never occurred to me that drinking might be something he could not control.

When the light went on inside me spiritually, and as I read and studied the Bible, other aspects of my life began to come into a new, clear focus. I realized that our financial situation was unstable. Grey still spent money like he always had but worked very little and had borrowed an extravagant amount to finance the farm operation. Our daughter Julia had just gotten married and had had an expensive wedding and reception. I began to wonder if my inheritance was supporting us. My greatest concern was that we would not have enough money to pay for Robert's and Debbie's college education. Fortunately, the other children were through college or almost finished with graduate school.

That was when I bucked the good-ol'-boy system for the first time. It was January 1982. When the next check from my father's trust came in and Grey handed it to me to sign, I said quite nicely, "Grey, I've decided that I'm going to keep this money. We may need it for the children's education." He said nothing, picked up the rest of his papers, and walked out of the room. A few weeks later he told me that he could not pay the bill for Julia's reception because I had not turned over my trust check to him. I signed the check over to him, sensing that my fears of financial disaster were real.

A month later, in February 1982, I arrived home from church on a cold Sunday evening. Grey said, "Sit down. I want to tell you something." I sat down and he continued in a flat tone of voice. "I've gotten a lawyer and I'm divorcing you. You'll not get anything. Everything is in my name."

I was unusually calm and asked, "Why? What do you plan to do with me?"

He said, "I want to start dating again." He had just gotten back from a vacation with the Capitol Investment Club and I had not accompanied him. His lawyer was a member of the Club. I felt deserted and sick to my stomach.

Unbeknownst to me, Grey had been building a case against me for some time. I knew of other husbands who had done this to their wives, having their lawyer and judge friends swiftly end the marriages and leave the wives with nothing. He was telling our grown children that I was a paranoid schizophrenic. He wrote a letter than insinuated that Julia and Craig, who were both married at the time, were having marital problems because of "my illness." Their spouses had thought they were marrying into this wonderful family, only to discover that their new mother-in-law was insane! They were all afraid to have children in case the problem was genetic (Craig was in medical school and Julia's husband was in his internship). Following is an excerpt from this letter Grey wrote to Craig and his wife dated August 4, 1983:

> *Your Mother and I have made several visits, both*
> *with a psychiatrist, Dr. Mary B. Wheatley, and a psy-*
> *chologist, Dr. Robert Hossford. In addition to this,*

*your Mother has taken numerous tests from Dr.
Wheatley, and the two of them not only agree that
there is no psychotic disorder at present, nor appar-
ently in the past, but are attesting to same in a letter
to that effect.*

*Unfortunately, for some 16 years, more or less, I
have been living with what obviously was a mis-
diagnosis that I sincerely believed. . . .*

Grey finally called Craig and his wife, Elizabeth, Robert,
Debbie, and me into our bedroom to apologize. (Julia and her
husband were living in New Orleans.) He admitted to giving
them false information concerning my mental and emotional
stability. What is interesting is that he claimed to have
received this "mis-diagnosis" sixteen years prior, but he had
never requested that I see a mental health person until we
began marriage counseling that year. The only conclusion I
can reach is that he made this up. It never occurred to me that
Grey would do this to me. After all, he needed me so desperately. I did everything for him and protected him. Why would
he ever want to get rid of me?

Believe it or not, after Grey made the announcement that
he was going to divorce me, we continued living together for
two years. At my request, the Presbyterian Church referred
us to a "Christian" counselor. Grey and I went together several times, then separately. Soon I was the only one going
because Grey insisted that he didn't need help. I discovered
that the counselor had been married three times and wasn't
surprised when he advised us to get a divorce. In the midst of
all this, our daughter Debbie became so troubled that she also

131

began seeing a counselor.

Grey encouraged me to get an attorney and recommended some, but by that time I had enough sense to know I had to find someone outside his legal circle, someone I could trust. Grey was so completely and powerfully connected in the legal community, that this was a big problem. So I found a female attorney in Jackson who agreed to take my case even though I had no access to the money that was rightfully mine, including my inheritance from my father. She began an aggressive investigation of Grey's assets and he found out about it. He came to me immediately and begged me to "start over." He claimed that he had acted rashly because of the stresses of our financial situation.

I confronted him with the fact that he had spread rumors about me being unstable to the children and some of our friends, and that much of my inheritance had been invested in properties and gas leases and such that were in his name only. He admitted all of this and said he was sorry. As a show of good faith, not only would he pay my attorney's fee, but he would put the plantation home and 2.88 acres of the surrounding land in my name alone and give me clear title to our wedding gifts and silver. Then we would go on a second honeymoon and everything would be different. He actually did all these things, and later he even wrote a letter of apology and explanation to our children. I believed I could trust him again.

We went to Point Clear, but he kept himself so drugged that he slept most of the time. He was extremely depressed. When we returned home it was "same song, second verse." He continued giving me a weekly allowance, and now I was to give his secretary a written report that she would type up and give him to review. But there was one major difference, and that difference was I.

I had found hope and peace in the Lord. My new relationship with Him gave me a strength and understanding I had never known. I was no longer afraid of the future, and I had a boldness about my faith that would carry me through this trial and the trials to come. I had finally realized that my protection and provision in life did not come from my father, my husband, my children, or any other human being. Everything I needed came from God—and I refused to give up hope.

CHAPTER 17

DEBBIE

Grey and I continued living together on the plantation. There were many nights when I would drive him to the hospital because he was certain he was having a heart attack. There were a number of major surgeries—two aneurysms, two hernias, both carotid arteries—and taking him to Jocyln Clinic in Boston because his diabetes was out of control. His depression was so prevalent that I wondered if anything the doctors did was really helping. He was increasingly violent, losing his temper at the slightest upset, throwing things and slamming doors.

By now all the children had left home but two, Robert and Debbie. Robert had just finished the tenth grade and Debbie the ninth. They were terribly unhappy, and I was convinced that they needed to get out of the awful environment at the plantation. When we had first moved there, Grey had said that he would drive the children into Jackson every day for school, as that was where his office was. Then he would pick them up and bring them home, and we would have nice, long evenings together.

However, he only kept this promise for a little over two weeks.

He soon built an office for himself at the plantation, and the daily drive to school was left to me. The plantation was about 45 miles to Jackson, so I drove nearly 180 miles every day. After awhile, I realized this was not going to work because the children hated it as much as I did. We knew the schools were not good in Vicksburg, which was nearer, so I asked Grey for permission to enroll Robert in McCallie School in Chattanooga, Tennessee, the boarding school he had attended. He gave me permission to do so but said that I would have to figure out a way to pay for it because he wouldn't.

Robert and I drove to Chattanooga and I was able to get him into McCallie by begging. I literally got on my knees and said, "You've got to help me. I don't have any money. This child needs an education. His father is drunk and depressed all the time, and he needs to get into an environment that will give him a chance. Please, can you do something?" The head-master was shocked but compassionate. He said that they would find a way to help me, and they did. He obtained Robert's tuition from a number of private donors, and so Robert escaped the horrors of the plantation in 1982.

Next I had to find a safe place for Debbie. I tried to get her into a girl's boarding school in Memphis, but they wouldn't help me with the finances. Then I went to All Saints' Episcopal School in Vicksburg, where my sisters-in-law and nieces had attended, and asked for help. They would give some financial assistance but by no means all.

Desperate and knowing she loved her grandchildren, I went to see Mrs. Flowers. Through the years we had maintained a good relationship and had mutual respect for one another. She quickly gave me a check for $5,000. I told her I would try to pay her back someday, but she said, "Don't worry about it. I'll probably be dead by then." She asked me why Grey couldn't pay for Debbie's schooling, but I had no answer for her. Grey had paid my attorney before she could obtain a report on his assets, so I still had no idea what our financial situation was. Therefore, I didn't know if he couldn't or wouldn't pay for the children's schooling. I just had to accept that he wasn't going to take the responsibility.

Now I drove Debbie to school every day, but Vicksburg was only twelve miles from our home. The drive was easier, but she was still in the middle of this horrible turmoil at home. It was during her time at All Saints that she began smoking cigarettes and using drugs, including alcohol. I had no idea this was happening, but every morning I had a terrible time getting her up and dressed for school. She had frequent headaches and would beg not to go. The years of resistance to my affection now became outbursts of anger and rebellion. She began pitting Grey and me against each other to get her own way. I knew nothing about drugs, so her behavioral changes baffled me. Looking back, I wish I had been better informed.

Following is a letter I received from Debbie, which revealed the distress she was experiencing, for which I felt terrible guilt and responsibility.

Mom,

I'm writing this note separately because I have something more to say!

Well, remember when, just recently, you thought that maybe you and Dad would have to get a divorce? You remember Daddy spreading things around about you? Do you remember when he was over-dosing himself with medicine or drugs? Well, I do! I forgave him, but I will never, ever forget, no matter how hard I try to, I'll never forget. . . . During that period of time, I was always either in my room, the playroom, or outside crying, asking God, "Why does this have to happen to me?" I felt it was a lot of my fault and that it was yours and Dad's. I said "Why me?" but I thought that it was my fault. Things really started to get confusing to me. I didn't understand some things and didn't want to understand some things. Mom, this may not make much sense to you. I'm trying to be clear. I'm saying that even though all of that happened, I'll always love you, no matter how much you two argue, or no matter how much we argue. I'll always love you and Dad. Mom, I really got to admire you when you were going through that time, Dad spreading things, overdosing, and talk of divorce. You stuck it out. I really do love you because you were tough, but gentle. You felt hate and resentment, but you showed your love! Mom, I'm glad to have you for my mother! I love you! Very, Very Much!

Love always!

Debbie!

This letter was bittersweet. I was glad Debbie didn't blame me for everything and recognized her father's abnormal behavior, but I still felt terribly guilty that she was caught in this situation. Then one evening everything changed. I was sitting in the library doing my Bible study lesson, and Grey had gone into the kitchen for another drink. Suddenly I heard a deep, raspy voice behind me. I turned around and Grey's face was contorted and angry. The veins in his face and neck were distended and his eyes protruding. He said, "Someday I'll destroy you. I'll find some way to destroy you yet." This wasn't the man I knew—even drunk. He went on, "I can get away with anything, including murder." I was frozen with fear and did not move. He sat down at the library table, finished his drink, put his head down, and passed out.

I knew I had to get out of the house immediately. The next day I went into Jackson and told a couple of friends what had happened the night before. One friend was going to Hawaii for a month with her family and offered her home to Debbie and me. I gratefully accepted and went home to plan our escape.

A few days later, while Grey was away from the plantation (I had no idea where he was or how soon he would return), Debbie and I grabbed two paper bags each, packed what we could in them, got in my car, and then I recalled my friend Bunny DeCastelaine's escape from the Nazis. I ran back into the house and took all of my jewelry and my fur coat. Then Debbie and I drove into Jackson.

Debbie had long urged me to leave her father and take her with me, so she seemed relieved and much happier for a while. She had never wanted to leave Jackson and all of her friends to move to the plantation. Now we were back, safely housed in my friend's beautiful home, and Debbie seemed to be doing better.

Before my friend returned from Hawaii I found a cheap,

little apartment. A walk-up in a questionable neighborhood, it had a leaky roof and deep, dirty, yellow shag carpet. Nobody I knew would think that I would be living there. I asked for a six-month lease, and one day I walked into Grey's office at the plantation, past his two secretaries, and put the lease on the desk. I told him to sign it, and he did. Then I left without saying another word.

I telephoned Grey when I returned to Jackson and requested a bed for Debbie, one for Robert when he would come home from school, and one for me. I also asked for a few other things. He agreed. I asked my oldest son, who lived in Jackson, to get a truck and bring all these things to us from the plantation. His father gave him permission to do this.

I realized I had to find a way of supporting Robert, Debbie, and me. It was obvious to me that the men were making the significant money, and they were making it in the area of finance. Therefore, I contacted a very successful businessman (the one who had had to fire Grey years ago) and asked him to help me. He was wonderful. He gave me some tests, which revealed that I had a great talent for sales. He immediately started me in a course of study that would enable me to join his insurance and brokerage firm. I studied diligently day and night for several months.

The only study I had done in the last thirty years was my Bible Study, so these insurance courses were a daunting task. There were books, tapes, and huge loose-leaf notebooks that were full of information I had to learn. Sometimes I was so tired at night, I just stopped and cried. Then I felt better and would go back to studying. I had to keep going because quitting was not an option. I took one exam at a time until I had all the necessary credentials and licenses.

By the spring of 1984 I was able to join my friend's firm. I did IRA's, pensions, life insurance, and some health insurance. I never had call reluctance. I didn't mind anybody saying no because I knew the next person would probably say yes. Because I was paid strictly on commission, I was highly motivated! I enjoyed the work and helping people, so I began studying to get my brokerage license. Everything seemed better for a while.

Debbie's rebellious and angry behavior returned shortly after we moved into the apartment. She didn't like living in such poverty and her continuous complaints made our lives miserable. Eventually I took her to a Christian adolescent psychologist. She had Debbie tested for drugs, and that is when I found out how self-destructive she had become. Soon she had missed so much school that I had to place her in an education center. Grey paid for that. However, the counseling wasn't helping.

March 11, 1984, was Ettie's birthday and Debbie and I had made plans to drive to Vicksburg and take her to lunch. Debbie had asked to stop at the plantation for a moment. It was on our way, so we did. When we arrived, however, she informed me that she would not go with me to have lunch with Ettie, and that I could pick her up on my way back.

I had lunch with Ettie and was very embarrassed to tell her that her granddaughter did not want to celebrate her birthday with us. I returned to the plantation, and when I tried to open the back door it was locked. I knocked and no one came. I went to the front door and it was locked. Again I knocked and no one came. I went to a side door and it was open. By this time I knew something was wrong. I went through the kitchen and breakfast room into the main hall. On a round table in the center of the hall was a note. Before I picked it up I knew what it was. I was amazed at how calm I was.

Debbie had written that if she was gone, maybe her father and I would get back together again. Maybe she was the cause of all the problems. I thought, Where is she? and prayed, "God, help me." I sensed she would be on the master bed and found her there, completely unconscious. Now I cried out, "God, help me! Send someone to me!"

Just then the doorbell rang, and it was a young man I knew, a friend of Debbie's. To this day I have no idea why he was there because he knew she didn't live in the country anymore. I told him what had happened, and he helped carry Debbie to my car. As I strapped her in the seat, I instructed him to go find the drugs in her father's bathroom, make a list of them, call Baptist Hospital, and tell them to have everybody ready and waiting, that this was a suicide attempt. I would be there as fast as I could. I put cloths in the windows so they would flap in the breeze. I turned on the flashers and left to go as fast as I could into Jackson.

Before I reached the highway, Grey drove up beside me. I told him what was happening and he said, "Do you suppose I should follow you?"

I said, "I certainly would if I were you."

He said, "Well, I'll have to change clothes."

At this point nothing Grey did shocked me. I went on to the hospital.

The young man also called the Mississippi Highway Patrol

to escort me, but they never showed up. I raced to the hospital blowing my horn most of the way and finally arrived. Hospital personnel were ready for us and immediately forced charcoal down Debbie's throat. I called her Christian therapist, who came to the hospital right away. Grey arrived about an hour later dressed to the nines. He sat in the waiting room and said nothing.

When Debbie regained consciousness she refused to see me or Grey. She was furious with me for stopping her from killing herself. The therapist came to the waiting room and said to me, "I want you to go back there and apologize to Debbie for whatever you did that made her take those drugs."

In horror I said, "I will do no such thing. I never made her take those drugs. I'll go back and tell her I love her. I'll apologize for my part in the terrible circumstances she is in. But I never made her take those drugs. No, I will not tell her that. And I loved her enough to stop her."

The therapist became angry and told me I wasn't handling the situation correctly. Grey said nothing. I said nothing. And the therapist would only speak with Grey from that time on.

The hospital put Debbie in an isolation room with a nurse present at all times and a guard at the door. The only person she would see was her sister, my daughter Elizabeth. Years later Elizabeth told me that Debbie would just sit there and they never did much talking. Robert came home from school during that time and she agreed to see him, but she didn't talk to him either. Her other brothers and sister did not see her. Most of the family was embarrassed by her behavior and many didn't understand the seriousness of it, so they stayed in denial.

After she got out of the hospital, she repeatedly rebelled

against the rules that I established for her. She decided she couldn't handle the austerity of our life and went to live with her father. Then one day in church, the Presbyterian minister announced that a fifteen-year-old girl who was in an abusive situation needed a home. Good friends of mine volunteered and discovered that the girl was Debbie! They called me immediately because they knew the situation.

In the end Debbie went to live with a couple from the Presbyterian Church, the Howie family, and I prayed she was doing better. I called several times to talk to her, but each time Lee Howie said, "Well, I'll pray about it." Then he would never call back. Debbie soon went back to the plantation, however. Her father saw to it that she had whatever she wanted.

The following summer, when Robert was home from school, we received a telephone call from a desperate mother late one night. She said that Debbie was trying to kill her son and was on drugs. Robert and I rushed to her house and took Debbie to the closest hospital. She had overdosed again and the young man was trying to stop her from killing herself.

She refused to see us because she knew that we would try to stop her also. Right after we left the hospital, the mother of the boy she had attacked called us and said that if we didn't do anything about Debbie then she would have to file charges against her. I went before the judge with her and Robert and explained the situation to him. He signed committal papers to avert the possibility of criminal charges, and Debbie entered an alcohol and drug abuse rehabilitation center. The judge showed no real concern for her well-being, but the daughter of Grey Flowers could not be involved in such a scandal.

I had to face the fact that my beautiful daughter was now

a potential murderer. She was pretty, but she was also very tall and strong, and the drugs and alcohol made her homicidal as well as suicidal. I remember thinking to myself, "If she wants to kill herself, that's one thing, but I will not let her take another person's life."

Only parents who have dealt with a troubled child who is addicted to drugs, violent, and suicidal know the pain of it. I became numb. After years of being denied her affection and then the continuous rejection and disrespect, I had nothing left. I let her go. While in the rehabilitation center, she wrote a note to me, which I still have. The underlining and emphasis are hers.

I'm very happy to know that I'm not addicted according to my evaluation. I knew my tests would most likely turn out good; therefore, I would go home afterwards. But, I have thought and thought and prayed that I would be able to make myself get help. I know I have a problem. (AA) I prayed God would give me the right decision as of whether or not I should stay here after my test results came,—I've decided to stay for my 30 day or so stay. I pray I made the right decision. I feel I did. I'm scared but I'm willing to take time and try treatment—no matter what my tests are.

My main problem is <u>*Drinking*</u> *then* <u>*Drugs*</u>*—I would drink—then I couldn't stop. My main problem is that I can hardly resist alcohol. If someone was to offer me a beer or a scotch or something hard I would always take it. I slowed down a lot for several reasons. But, I know that if I were to leave and was* *given an opportunity to drink it would be hard to say no. My other problem—<u>Drugs</u>—is not so bad— I know I would most likely be able to put it aside but if I couldn't find a drink I'd take a drug. I will admit that I enjoy "SPEED." It would be hard to say no to it.*

When I would drink or use drugs I would never remember what I had said or done, afterwards. That scares me.

There's more to write but I'm sleepy it's 3:00 AM.

July 12, 1984
My B'day

<u>To My Parents!</u>

Thanks, for getting me here! I enjoy learning more and more about <u>AA</u> & <u>drugs</u>. I'm excited because I finally do see some hope. A lot of hope— and I am very happy. I would like to stay the remainder of the time, so would you please let me? <u>30 days</u>? I'm sorry Mother, Grey, & Clark for cussing ya'll out—I had my reasons then. But now I appreciate ya'll. Please forgive me, well, I need to go. I have more to write but can't. Love always to you—Dad & Mother & Family.

P.S. Please tell the Howies thanks for being true friends and I love them.

Debbie stayed in the center for the time she needed, then went to live with the Howie family. Again, she wanted nothing to do with Robert and me, but this time she began to get her life on track. She finished high school and went on to get a college degree.

Watching my daughter go through this horror opened up my eyes fully to the years of drinking. Until I quit drinking on doctor's orders, I did not really understand how destructive it was or that some people, like Grey and Debbie, could not take one drink and then stop. I noticed how so many in my generation were dissipated and families destroyed because of alcohol and the use of drugs (prescription and nonprescription).

I also understood this struggle to be free of an addiction because it wasn't until 1990 that I finally addressed my addiction to nicotine. I had stopped smoking several times, but identifying it as an addiction and going through three intense days of literally climbing the walls and praying finally set me free from cigarette smoking forever. The key was recognizing it as an addiction.

Finally, I watched helplessly as my own child sank lower and lower because of alcohol and drug addiction. Later I became aware that some of my other children had had problems with alcohol and drugs for a while. Thank God, they all came out of it.

CHAPTER 18

THE TIMEPIECE FLIES APART

When I left Grey nearly everyone but Robert and Debbie blamed me. Even Ettie and my sister became estranged to save face in Vicksburg, where Mrs. Flowers resided. I was doing this terrible thing to him and breaking up this wonderful, prestigious family. The most disturbing information came from Robert and Debbie, who told me that Grey had made it clear to the children that they would never see a dime of inheritance if they had any contact with me. For that reason, Debbie had a great struggle and eventually returned to the plantation. Only Robert stayed with me and never wavered.

Robert had become a Christian before he was out of elementary school and had shown strength of character from a very early age. When he was thirteen, he confronted the pastor of the Presbyterian Church about the fact that a man who was in prison for murder was still listed in the church bulletin as a deacon. The man in question had faked his death by burning an unidentified person in his car in order to get his life insurance and avoid paying his debts. He was later picked up in Atlanta, tried, convicted, and imprisoned just north of

Jackson. The pastor told Robert that it was the business of the church and nothing for him to be concerned about.

Later on but before I left, when Grey first announced to the children that he was going to divorce me, Robert told him that because he was a deacon, he should not be divorcing his wife of thirty-two years. If he insisted on doing so, he should step down as a deacon. This infuriated Grey, and from that time on Robert, who had always been Grey's favorite, was singled out as a traitor. When his father's sister died and left a lot of money to the children, Robert received nothing. He was virtually kicked out of the family and had no contact with his brothers and sisters for years. When his father passed away in 1990, Robert was excluded from the will. His father had disinherited him. He paid a terrible price for standing up for what he believed to be right.

Along with Robert, there were a few of my friends who knew exactly what I was going through and stuck with me through thick and thin. And then two of Grey's friends began to realize what was really going on. After I left Grey, he had become unkempt and would miss his insulin shots. They soon realized he was an alcoholic and that he needed treatment badly. Like me, they were especially concerned because of the diabetes.

It is interesting to me, as I look back, that these two friends were not drinkers. All of our other social friends were, and many of them were alcoholics who went in for treatment. It seems that high society and drinking go hand-in-hand in so many cities in America. And then we wonder why so many of our children and grandchildren are addicted to hard drugs.

In July of 1984 I signed papers committing Grey to an

alcohol and drug rehabilitation center, hoping he would get the help he needed. Judge Paul Alexander wrote in his Order that he had received "clear and convincing proof that the Respondent (Grey Flowers) is under the influence of alcohol or drugs to the extent that if Respondent is served with process Respondent will, in all likelihood, flee the jurisdiction of the Court or physically harm Respondent or others, and Respondent should be committed and confined, without notice, until a hearing, to a suitable private facility for the treatment of chemically dependent persons."

Robert and I began attending an evening class at the hospital for families of those who were chemically dependent. That's when I discovered that I was a first-class enabler. Ironically, a few months before I left Grey, I had heard Mrs. Flowers say, "I'll never have to worry about Grey because as long as Anne is alive she'll take care of him." While I was living with Grey, I had seen to all of his needs. I gave him his insulin shots, monitored his medication, took him to the doctor, saw to it that he was well dressed and fed, bought his alcohol and cigarettes—and lied for him. I hid him and his problems from the world and our children.

We learned that a family of an alcoholic and/or drug addict is like a finely tuned timepiece. When one part steps out of the system, refusing to enable or skirt the truth any longer, the whole watch flies apart. At first it seems like what you've done is horrible, and everyone involved will tell you that. But eventually you see that the only way the truth can be known and people's lives saved is for someone to stop the watch from ticking. I was that someone, and when I had left Grey, the timepiece that was our family had begun to fly apart.

Grey agreed to meet his two friends at Humana Hospital in Jackson. With a doctor who was also a recovering alcoholic, they confronted him with his drinking problem. Then they asked, "Do you realize you have a problem?" Grey said yes. When asked if he would stay for treatment, he said, "Yes, but not now. I have some things to do first. I will come back later." Then his friends and the doctor presented the committal papers to him. He began cursing and they had to subdue him to admit him. They kept him that night and gave him some tests the next day. The tests showed that his body was dependent upon drugs and alcohol and severely damaged.

According to hospital procedure, the patient cannot make a telephone call for three days. However, Grey bribed an orderly so that he could call one of our sons. He told him to call my sister's husband, Judge Bullard, to tell him where he was and get him out immediately.

Other than Robert (and Debbie for a while), our children never questioned anything their father told them to do. The fear of his disapproval and anger was so great that they just did whatever he ordered. Our son dutifully called his uncle, who called Judge Alexander and "requested" that he rescind his Judgement of Committal. Judge Alexander complied and no one was notified but the hospital. Grey was released that night, but his two friends and I were unaware of it.

Late that same night someone began banging on my door and shouting. Robert and a friend of mine were with me. I did not open the door but asked who it was. Grey yelled, "Open the damn door. I want the keys to my car." His two friends had given me his car keys, and I had moved his car from the hospital to one of my friend's garages for safe-keeping. Before I could open the door, Grey and our son broke the lock and forced the door open. A section of the door splintered in the process.

"Where the hell did you put my keys?" Grey shouted.

"I'm not going to tell you, but I will get your car for you," I answered.

Grey turned to our son and said, "Get those keys from him if he's got them."

Our son grabbed Robert and began to assault him as he tried to locate the keys. Fortunately, my friend stepped forward and screamed for him to stop. Grey recognized her and immediately ordered him to stop. My friend happened to be one of the most influential people in Mississippi. In the meantime I called the police, but Grey and our son left before they got there.

When the police arrived they asked if we wanted to press charges. I said yes. They warned me, "If you press charges and he's arrested, when he gets out he could come back and kill you. We can't promise to protect you. That's just the way domestic violence is."

I was reminded of the time I had called the Sheriff's office when I was still living at the plantation. Grey had been violent and I had been frightened. I wanted them to arrest him, thinking that at least it would get him out of the house, and spending a few nights in jail might cause him to recognize how extreme his behavior had become. The officers had told me then, "With his connections, we couldn't keep you safe." (This sheriff, by the way, ruled Warren County with an iron fist for many years. Finally, in 1996 the Mississippi Supreme

Court decided he could not remain in office because of his felony convictions.)

Now I bitterly told the policemen, "Never mind, then." My fear was turning to anger that the hospital had not called to warn me that Grey had been released. I woke up the apartment manager, who replaced the door that same night. My friend left quite shaken, but I was grateful to God that she happened to be there that night. Her presence and courage might have saved Robert's life, and now someone else besides Robert, Debbie, and I knew how violent Grey Flowers could be. The timepiece was definitely flying apart.

I remained haunted by Grey's words that he would find a way to destroy me. To be safe, Robert and I left the apartment the next morning for a friend's home in another section of town. We hid for a month, waiting for things to cool down. I mailed Grey's car keys to him after I moved his car to my apartment parking lot and Robert and I were safely hidden. My own car was always in my friend's garage. This home had been used a number of times for women in distress.

The legal system had dealt me a terrible blow, and to this day I blame it for the divorce that became inevitable because Judge Alexander would not stand by his ruling. I believe that if he had, Grey may have received the help he needed, and we may have been able to keep our family together. As it was, with Grey refusing medical help and counselors advising us to divorce, I knew I had to file for divorce and try to get a fair settlement—a nearly impossible feat for a wife in Mississippi.

CHAPTER 19

WHERE'S ANNE SHARP?

In the fall of 1984, my mother flew into Jackson to visit her ailing aunt in Greenville. Her cousin picked her up at the airport, and they proceeded west on I-20. I did not know that she had kept track of me through the years, and she stopped to visit me at our plantation. When she rang the doorbell, Grey came to the door and was surprised to see her. She explained her mission to see her aunt and asked, "Where's Anne Sharp?"

Grey answered, "She's left me."

"Why did she leave you?" my mother asked.

"I don't know. Why don't you ask her?" He shut the door.

I received a telephone call from Ettie several days after that. She said, "Anne Sharp, I just got a call from your sister. Your mother is staying with her and wants to come see you and spend the night with you."

I said, "Ettie, how can I do that? I don't even know her."

She said, "Well, you just have to do it, that's all."

"But what will we talk about? And I live in such a trap of

a place. I won't know what to do."

She responded, "Just go to the tennis courts at Millsaps at 2:30 on Saturday. She will meet you there."

Then I asked, "How will I know her? What does she look like now?" It had been over twenty years since my grandmother's funeral, and I could not remember her face.

Ettie paused and said slowly, "Oh, you'll know her all right."

Millsaps College is in Jackson, and Robert had decided to attend school there in order to be near me. Grey refused to pay for his once-favorite-son's education because he was still having contact with me. However, Robert received scholarship money, did odd jobs, and I was able to supply the rest of it.

I was working full-time for the insurance and investment firm, but my income was still small because I was paid on commission only and I was so new at it. Friends gave me clothing, pots and pans, silverware, and we ate off old TV dinner dishes. One of my friends was a Doncaster representative in New Orleans. She would box up her discarded clothing and send it to me. And so I maintained a decent wardrobe. Still, with my fashionable and sophisticated mother coming to visit, I felt totally inept. The idea of her spending the night in my little apartment on "the wrong side of town" was so intimidating that I simply had to trust God that it would work out.

I wore one of my best Doncaster suits and donned sunglasses when I went to meet her. The sunglasses gave me the feeling that I could hide. I arrived at the tennis courts at Millsaps College and saw no one for a few minutes. Then I looked to my left and saw a very beautiful, well-dressed woman walking toward me. As she got closer, she smiled and

I knew that she was my mother. Even though I had had a brief encounter with her at my grandmother's funeral in 1962, I felt like it was the first time I had ever really looked at her.

She said, "Hello darlin'," and hugged me warmly. "I'm looking forward to spending the night with you." Unlike our meeting at my grandmother's funeral, I was immediately put at ease.

My sister had driven her to Millsaps, so we walked over to her car. I greeted Betty, who said nothing, and we put our mother's luggage in my car. As Betty drove away Mother said, "Before we get started, I have to go to the ladies' room. Where's the nearest one?"

I took her to Robert's dormitory. It was Saturday and the campus was deserted because of a football game, and I knew the boys would be gone. We walked in and it was dark except for a light at the right side of the lobby. A familiar deep voice called out, "Mother, what are you doing here?"

I was thrilled that for some reason Robert had decided not to go to the game. "Come here, Robert. I want you to meet your grandmother."

My mother hugged him and said again, "Before we go any further, please show me where the ladies' room is."

While she was gone Robert and I talked about how wonderful it was that God had arranged this meeting. Our faith was a strong bond between us. When mother returned Robert said that he would go with us in order to carry his grandmother's bags up the stairs to my apartment. In the car, she turned to him and said, "I want to give my grandson something." She handed him several twenty-dollar bills. Robert was extremely grateful. More than that, he was completely charmed.

My mother acted like my tacky little apartment was a palace. I had never met anyone with such poise. She made Robert and me feel completely at ease. A friend brought us some sandwiches and soup to eat for dinner, then Robert returned to school. The two of us talked until we saw light coming through the curtains

"How did you know I was here?" I asked. She told me about going to the plantation and her conversation with Grey.

Then she asked, "Why did you leave him?"

I told her that he had threatened to destroy me, that he had said he could get away with murder. She stated emphatically, "That's pure hatred." After a short pause she said, "Do you have a good lawyer? Have you put in for temporary support?"

I said, "I have filed for it, but the judge has refused to even look at the papers." The judge was my brother-in-law, Judge Nat Bullard.

Mother said, "He's got to do it!"

"Mother, you're in Mississippi. A judge is very powerful and does what he wants to do. It has nothing to do with the law." My recent experiences with Judges Alexander and Bullard had taught me that lesson.

"Well, that's ridiculous. That's wrong." I wondered if some of my sensitivity to injustice might be inherited from my mother.

Getting to know her was like looking at my past, present, and future all at once. Not knowing her all these years was like hopping around on one leg. Although my father had always spoken well of my mother and her family, I was discovering an entire family tree, half of me that had been a mystery was unfolding before my eyes.

I looked like her. We had the same mannerisms when we spoke. Although I had quit smoking for a period of time, in the stress of the divorce I had started again, and we held our cigarettes the same way. We held our coffee cups the same way. Our personalities were so similar. Neither one of us assessed blame or hurt to the other for the past. Both of us were easy-going, liked people, laughed a lot, and generally trusted too easily. We enjoyed the same activities. Our voices were alike in tone and inflection. We mirrored each other, even though we had spent little time together. I was 53 and she was 72.

She told me about her life, the good and the bad. Most touching was her account of leaving me when I was a baby. She had gone upstairs to my aunt and uncle's room, where I was asleep in my crib. I was lying on my tummy, and she had leaned over to kiss me. My tiny feet were sticking out from my gown, and she had wept as she had said goodbye. For years she was haunted by my little feet, often having night-mares about them. I sensed in her both courage and regret, and there was also relief that she and I were finally coming to an understanding of one another.

I was overwhelmed. At a time when most friends and loved ones had turned against me, God sent my natural mother to encourage and support me. It was a time of heal-ing for her, for me, and for Robert. He too was being shunned and was hungry for the love and acceptance that he received from his grandmother. It gave us a warm sense of family at a time when we needed it most.

When we saw the sun coming up, we quickly jumped in bed to get two hours of sleep. Then she asked to see my other children. I told her about Debbie and that the others didn't want to see me either. She said, "Call them anyway and tell them I want them here." Craig was out of town, but Julia and her husband and baby, Elizabeth, Robert, and Debbie came. They all stayed a short while, and Mother made it very pleasant.

I received a telephone call that evening from Julia, who said sarcastically, "Well, now we think we understand you. You're just like your mother." I think she was probably referring to the fact that my mother had left my father also. This was a bitter moment for me. Except for Robert, it was like the forces of evil had pulled a black curtain over my children's eyes so that they could not see the truth.

Mother spent another night, and the next day she wanted all of us to take her back to her cousin's home in Brandon, Mississippi. Debbie had her own car and followed us. We had a pleasant visit with my mother's cousin, and she bought Robert and Debbie some clothes. She also purchased a few things for me. Debbie left first, but before Robert and I departed Mother said, "We will stay in touch from now on. And I want you to come see me and my husband, Gus, in Florida." We hugged and kissed each other good-bye, and Robert and I returned to Jackson.

Meeting my mother was a turning point in my life, and from that time on we were very close. We called frequently and I visited her at her home in Coral Gables, Florida, on several occasions. She had not remarried until after my father had married Ettie. Her marriage to Gus, who was twenty years younger than she, had lasted a long time and was a very happy one.

For spring break she flew Robert to Florida for a visit. I had to work and couldn't go. He had a wonderful time and she thoroughly enjoyed him. Then December 2, 1987, I received a telephone call from my mother's sister, Aunt Nancy, who said, "Gus has died and your mother needs you. Get here as soon as you can."

I made arrangements at work and called Robert, who was taking his last exam for the term in four days. After the exam we left for Florida. We drove through the night and arrived the next day. Mother was devastated over Gus' death. Because he was so much younger, this was a complete shock. She cried and cried, "It wasn't supposed to be like this. Fourteen years is too short."

We comforted her the best we could and made the time a little easier for her. Then one day she looked at me and said, "I could never understand why you married Grey Flowers." She paused, then went on, "He must have been awfully good in bed."

I was taken aback and laughed.

She went on. "I've known Grey and his family for years."

It was like someone had just struck me in the face. "Mother, what do you mean?" I asked incredulously.

"I used to go to Vicksburg all the time after your father and I divorced. I dated several men there and went to a lot of the parties. I'd see Grey and we would dance together."

I was shocked. "He's never, ever mentioned your name. Whenever I talked about you, he acted like he had never seen or heard of you."

Now she looked shocked. "I can't believe that."

I continued, "None of his sisters or his mother mentioned that they knew you either."

She said, "That's ridiculous. His mother and my mother were roommates in college at Sophie Newcomb in New Orleans."

"You mean, Mrs. Flowers . . ."

"Of course. Mrs. Flowers and Ma were roommates."

"But Mrs. Flowers has never said a word about it!" I cried. I thought back to the wonderful conversations I had had with Mrs. Flowers when we met and through the years.

Mother said, "Well, I can understand why. My mother had beautiful clothing and jewelry and a lot of it was stolen from her room. My grandmother went to the headmistress to find out why these things were missing. When they conducted a search they found the missing items in Hester Flowers' trunks. Hester was asked to leave."

"Oh, then that's why she never finished college!" I gasped.

She said, "Yes. No wonder they kept you in the dark. When I was in Vicksburg Grey carried on and wanted to be around me, but I would have nothing to do with him. I just didn't like him. In fact, that's why I never contacted you even after we met at Ma's funeral. If you were happy with him, I didn't want to mess it up. There was too much history there."

The mystery was unraveling. The realization that my mother and I were so much alike in looks and personality made me wonder if my husband had ever really loved me.

Was he chasing his fantasy of Mother? And was his mother trying to get revenge for the exposure of her transgression in college?

The memory of how we met, how I was courted, how quickly he proposed, how dreamily he looked at me, and how passionate and yet in some way detached he was in lovemaking—all this made perfect sense in light of what my mother was telling me. All the years of sensing that something was wrong in our marriage, long before the onset of encephalitis, came into clear focus. For the first time in my life, I understood and felt the full agony of deception and betrayal.

Mother said, "I don't understand how you couldn't know about these things. Ettie and your sister knew."

That was the fatal blow. My heart tightened and my stomach was suddenly queasy. I managed to whisper, "They never even told me that you visited them. I don't understand how they could have done this to me."

She answered, "Don't you realize they've always been jealous of you?" She waited a few moments and then asked, "Anne Sharp, have you ever been jealous?"

"Mother, I don't think I've ever had anything to be jealous about."

She threw her head back and laughed. "Neither have I."

CHAPTER 20

DREAMS, MIRACLES, AND FORGIVENESS

During the time I lived in that strange, little apartment on the wrong side of Jackson, I went through some of the greatest torment and turmoil I believe a human being can experience. When Robert was with me, he went through it too. The daylight hours weren't so bad. All of us in that apartment complex were going through hard times. We would sit on the steps and visit. None of us had much, so we often shared what we had. Everyone there wore second-hand clothing, and I learned where and how to get the best. One little boy needed an operation badly, but his parents had no insurance or money to pay for it. I called a couple of my wealthy friends, and they responded immediately. That was one time I knew I had been put in that horrible part of town for a reason.

The nights were different. There were many nights that I went to sleep with a pillow over my head to drown out the yelling and fighting and cursing. I could sense the terrible unhappiness all around me, and it was not uncommon to wake up the next morning and find that someone in the apartment a few doors down had been beaten, raped, or murdered. One man threw his live-in girlfriend off the second-story balcony. But as time went on I got used to it, made friends, and stayed there over four years.

To this day, it makes me sick to my stomach when I remember how Grey used his power and prestige to harass me and Robert when he was there. Wherever we drove in Jackson, somebody followed us. Often, either late at night or in the early hours of morning, police cars would pull up outside our door, lights flashing. We would be awakened to heavy beating on the door (they never used the doorbell). When we opened the door, we stared into the faces of intimidating policemen, guns at their sides, who served me and sometimes Robert with some kind of summons to appear in court. It was humiliating and demoralizing. Through all of this, however, my faith in God grew stronger, and He came through for me again and again.

One of the ways God spoke to me was through dreams, which have always fascinated me. Most of my life, I have not had dreams. I simply go to bed, fall asleep, and awake without any memory of a dream. There were a few nightmares when I was very little. Daddy called them "dog dreams." They usually happened after we saw a movie about cowboys and Indians. I would dream that the Indians were chasing me on their ponies and wake up frightened.

I would quietly tiptoe down the hall of the boarding house or hotel to Daddy's room, and as I told him all about it, he would get out the chocolate-covered marshmallow cookies, which he always kept in the closet. After we had a great feast of them and he had reassured me, he would put me in bed with him and I would sleep peacefully. The dog dreams were few and far between, but because of the cookies, I always wished I had had more.

It seems that I didn't dream at all until after I left Grey and moved into Jackson. Then I had a series of dreams that warned me about things to come or told me things I had no way of knowing but would need to know. The dreams were so unusual because they were clear and detailed. I wrote each of them down, but there is one that stands out above all others.

One night I was awakened by a loud voice calling, "Anne! Anne!" I sat right up and heard it say again, "Anne!" Whether it was audible or not, I didn't know. But I heard it. Then I looked at the clock. It was three o'clock in the morning.

I said to the Lord, "What is this?"

I heard a calm voice inside me say, "I want you to call Linda tomorrow morning at a quarter to six and ask her about Centreville Realty Company." Then I went right back to sleep. Linda was a young mother whom I had met at the All Saints' Episcopal Church Bible study in South Jackson. She was divorced and was moving with her three children to Sewanee, Tennessee, to attend seminary and become a priest.

The next morning I awakened at quarter to six. I picked up the phone and dialed Linda's number. When she answered, I said, "Linda, I'm sorry it's so early, but I feel like I'm supposed to call you at this time."

"It's okay," she said, "I've been praying for you for fifteen minutes.

"Well, I'm supposed to ask you about Centreville Realty Company," I said.

"That's interesting because I grew up in Centreville and

know everything about that company. It's a holding company for oil lease properties." Then she gave names of people I could contact there. I wrote them down, we said goodbye, and I went back to sleep. That's when I had the following dream.

I was driving in Jackson, approaching the Merrill Lynch building. I had never gone into that building before, but there was a parking place right in front for me. I parked, got out of the car, put some money in the meter, and walked into the building. There was a nicely decorated atrium and two elevators in the back. I got on one and pushed the button for the third floor. At the third floor I got out of the elevator and turned left, then made an immediate right. I proceeded to the third door, opened it, and then I awoke.

After I awoke from the dream, I knew I had to act on it right away. I dressed and ate breakfast, then headed for the Merrill Lynch building. Sure enough, there was a parking place right where I had seen it in my dream. When I walked into the building, the atrium was exactly like I had dreamed with the two elevators at the back. I got in one and went to the third floor, where I turned left and then right, and opened the third door.

It was an office of some sort and a woman asked if she could help me. I said, tentatively, "Does anyone here know anything about Centreville Realty Company?" Just as I was speaking a very well-dressed woman entered the room and overheard my inquiry.

She came toward me and asked, "What is your name?"

"Anne Flowers."

"Come with me," she said warmly but firmly.

She led me into her office and I looked around. Against the

wall, below some windows, was a draftsman's desk with large maps on it. She said, "I've been waiting for you to come see me." Then she showed me a series of oil lease properties that were in Grey's name. She said, "I shouldn't be telling you this, but you have a right to know. You're being taken to the cleaners. Yesterday your husband received a payment of $64,380.00 for these oil leases."

I remembered that in 1967 Grey had used some of my inheritance to purchase oil leases. They were to be set aside for our retirement. It turned out that he never filed the deeds at the courthouse until nearly twenty years later, 1986, just after he filed his countersuit for divorce against me. At that time he put the oil leases in his name only.

I was very grateful to this woman for giving me this information, which she couldn't have without me soliciting it. The very next day I was served with a summons to appear in Chancery Court the following day. I was not told what this was about or given any filings concerning the matter. I was representing myself at the time, and when I appeared I was handed the motion filed by Grey's attorney. I immediately asked the judge for a postponement, as I had had no time to review the documents. He denied my request.

Glancing through the paperwork, it seemed that Grey was attempting to break an agreement he and I had signed concerning the distribution of the proceeds from the sale of Ceres Plantation. He had asked me to meet him at the University Club one day and the agreement was typed and ready for both of us to sign. The property was sold for $1,800,000, and since the main house and 2.88 acres were in my name, $625,000 was legally mine. However, after $1,112,106.36 in debts and taxes were paid, that left an equity of $677,893.64. The agreement gave me $208,000, and Grey divided some of the rest among our children. If I had maintained my claim on the part of the property in my name and sold it, after taxes and debts were paid I would have received $320,000.00. So Grey got a very good deal with me agreeing to take only $208,000. The motion I was handed now alleged that this transaction was illegal, that I had forced Grey to sign the agreement under duress, and that he should only have to pay me $63,000.

I glanced over my shoulder, praying for God to give me wisdom. Robert and my friends Dean and Peter were with me in the courtroom, and I noticed several beautifully dressed black people walk in and sit in the fourth row on my side. Men and women. They were lovely looking people, but I did not know who they were. Dean turned to Robert and said, "Go back there and ask them to pray for your mother."

When Robert made that request, they said to him, "That's why we're here."

He came back and told Dean and Peter, and they all turned around and smiled at them. I was sitting by myself at the defendant's desk and did not hear Robert's report. However, I glanced back again and noticed that everybody on my side of the courtroom was praying and everybody on the other side was mumbling to each other (including my other children). There was a whole battery of attorneys over there and I was alone.

When the time came for me to cross-examine Grey, something amazing happened. He admitted that he had initiated the meeting to distribute the funds from the sale of the plantation, that he had in no way been coerced, and that he had typed up the agreement that we both signed! But that was not the end of the miracle. Because the motion his attorney had filed dealt with the distribution of marital assets, I was able to ask him a battery of questions concerning his purchase of oil leases in 1967, using assets I brought to the marriage. Grey's face grew more flushed and his countenance more angry with each inquiry. By the time I asked him whether or not he had recently received a check in the amount of $64,380.00, he was furious—and there was nothing his attorney could do about it.

When the issue had been heard, Judge Moss said that he was going to go back to his chambers and review it. Grey's attorney asked if he could come over and speak to me to see if we could make a deal. The judge told us to go ahead, that he would be in his chambers.

The attorney came over to me and said, "Would you take a hundred and twenty-five thousand to settle this."

I said no and he asked me why not. I said, "Well, because the full amount and more belongs to me."

He went back to his side and then came back again and said, "Well, would you take a hundred and forty thousand and we'll settle this?"

I said no.

He said, "Don't you realize you could lose everything?"

I said, "How can I lose everything? I don't have anything to lose."

He said, "Oh," and went back to his side again.

About ten minutes later, Judge Moss came out and pronounced me the victor. He denounced the opposing attorney and told him to never bring a motion like that into his court again.

We turned around to thank the people who had come to pray for us. They were gone. The deputy by the back door, which was the only entrance to the courtroom except through the judge's chambers, said that he had never let them out. They had never gone past him. The judge was in his chambers and said he had not seen them. They had totally disappeared. Where they came from, I don't know. But I have always referred to them as my black angels. God has such a great sense of humor. If they had been white people, the judge would have asked them to leave. That's why God sent black people to come to the court and pray for me. Nobody had the courage to ask them to leave because it would have caused a racial stir. I still have a good laugh about that one!

After I won the motion, the opposing attorney, Thomas Crockett, came over to me and said, "Anne, you can represent me any day." The next day he dissolved his law firm and got out of the practice of law. It was one of the largest law firms in the city, and he just closed it down. Several months later he came up to me at the church I was attending, St. Andrew's Episcopal Church, and apologized profusely for what had taken place. He asked if I could forgive him, and I said that I had already done so. My diligence to forgive quickly had been a lesson well learned, and it involves another amazing miracle God did for me during this dark time of my life.

Late in February of 1985 I had found a lump in my left breast. My doctor in Jackson did a mammogram, which showed abnormalities. I remembered a friend of mine, Lydy, saying, "If I ever had cancer, I would go straight to Anderson Clinic in Houston." I called her and she paved the way for me to get an appointment there right away.

Anderson did thorough testing on me and said they would notify me. I went right back to Jackson because I had to work. They sent me a letter stating that the growth was malignant. A wave of fear came over me as I realized that not only did I have a life-threatening problem, but the cancer insurance policy I had had for four months had elapsed. I had been unable to make the payment. I had no money. No insurance. And I did not have time to deal with this because I had to work to support Robert and myself.

The young man who had sold me the policy heard of my situation and called me. He said, "If you pay the premium now, I might be able to slip it through."

I was stunned when I said, "I will think about it." I thought about it long and hard because I was tempted, but I knew this was wrong. In the end, the way I handled this situation revealed to me how important integrity is—not just remaining honest with people and the law, but keeping my heart right with God.

First, I turned this nice young man down on his offer. Then I turned to God and said, "Okay, God. You said that by Jesus' stripes, I was healed." I read that verse of Scripture over my body, put my back against the wall, and said, "I'm jumping off this diving board with you, Lord. I'm not letting go of you. I'm trusting you all the way. And I'm not going to look back. I will not doubt." I talked to God like a good friend and told Him that no matter what happened, it wouldn't change our relationship.

Just then God showed me something. To my surprise, I had become a bitter woman. I saw that I was furious that the Mississippi judicial system was corrupt and Grey was a part of that corruption. I was enraged that after thirty-two years of marriage, my husband had complete control of our finances and our children because he was a wealthy, powerful man and no one dared come against him. And then there was the little matter of him knowing my mother before we were married, of his mother's relationship with my grandmother, and none of this being told to me.

I had left him for fear of my life and still attempted to help him with his alcoholism. For this, I found myself on the outside of the society of which I had been a great part all my life. Very few of my friends from the country club, the Junior League, and the Presbyterian Church continued to associate with me. The pastor of the church suggested that I attend another because Grey was still a deacon there.

The worst heartache was that all of my children but Robert had turned against me. Grandchildren were being born, and I would learn about it at the grocery store. Someone would say, "Oh, I know you're just thrilled over the new baby! How many does that make?" I would cover the pain with some inane remark like, "Oh, they're multiplying!" Then I would see little blonde children playing on a playground and wonder if they were my grandchildren. I didn't even know what they looked like.

Now I had cancer, no money, and my sister's husband, who was the judge in our divorce case, was doing everything he could to keep me from a fair hearing. Ettie and my sister had hidden things from me because of their jealousy. All these years I thought they loved me, and now even they had turned against me. I was deeply bitter because of my situation.

I grabbed my Bible angrily. It opened to the part that says that if you don't forgive others, God can't forgive you. Now I was really mad. I cried, "God, you know what Grey Flowers has done to me! He's deceived me. He's got control of my money. He's turned our children against me. I don't see my grandchildren. I'm disgraced. I'm lied about. You know what's happened. It's wrong!"

He said, "I know."

And I said, "Well, how can I forgive him?"

He said, "I did."

I said, "But you're God. How am I going to do this?"

Just then the word "obedience" came to me. I remembered the scripture that God prefers obedience over sacrifice. Suddenly it was very clear to me that I simply had to obey His Word and trust Him for the rest. So at three o'clock in the morning in that little, dumpy apartment, I got down on my knees. I had never gotten on my knees before, but this was really serious. With my Bible in my hands I read out loud that if you don't forgive others, God won't be able to forgive you. I said, "God, this is what it says, and you're going to have to help me. I'm going to do this in obedience to you, but I'm lying. And I want you to know that I know that I'm lying. I don't want to forgive any of them. But I've got to do it. I can't live with this bitterness."

I heard, "Open your mouth." Hesitantly, I opened my mouth and He provided the words for me to forgive. God is so good! As I spoke forgiveness toward everyone and everything that had hurt me, I felt a terrible weight lift off of me. When I got up, I was not angry anymore. I was free. Bitterness had no hold on me, and I knew I never had to be bitter again. It was the most wonderful thing that had ever happened. The Word of God had set me free.

The Word of God also opened my eyes to see that while a sensitivity to injustice is good, it must be tempered with forgiveness and wisdom. The gift that God had given me—to hate injustice and to do everything I could to see that truth prevailed—could easily have destroyed me if I had refused to also walk in forgiveness toward those who were doing wrong. I had come face to face with the challenge to be like Jesus, who hung on the cross—unjustly—and forgave all of us for putting Him there.

This new freedom and understanding was wonderful, but I endured another serious test of integrity. I had written a health insurance policy for the son of a good friend, who was home for the holidays and returning to his job in Europe. I had included in the policy that he would be out of the country, but when a claim for $900.00 came in, the insurance company refused to pay it. They stated that they could not cover a claim that occurred out of the United States.

I argued and fought to find some way of getting the company to pay this claim, and my boss said that he would see what he could do. I went back to my apartment and prayed, asking God what to do. Within minutes I knew I had to back up my word. God kept His Word to me and I had to keep my word to this young man. I turned to Robert and said, "If the company doesn't pay, I'll send him money." He agreed it was the right thing to do, even though money was extremely tight.

Three weeks later the company paid the claim, and after four-and-a-half months of declaring "by His stripes I was healed," in the fall of 1985 I no longer felt the lump in my breast. I went back to visit my doctor in Jackson, and the mammogram confirmed that it was gone. I was totally awestruck at what had happened. If I had trusted the insurance and the medical doctors, lied about the cancer policy, and continued being bitter, there was no doubt in my mind that I would have died and never received this amazing miracle of healing—in my emotions and my body.

When God freed me from the bitterness, He also reminded me of the blessings I did have, especially Robert. He had paid a heavy price for staying with me. The Lord knew I needed him and a few miracles to encourage me in what turned out to be the longest running divorce case in Mississippi history. In the many years of fighting for a fair and just settlement of property and assets, for example, there were five judges with whom I had to contend. I got to where I would pray, "God, renew them or remove them!" It was a biblical prayer—and it worked.

Remember Judge Alexander? After the horrible ramifications of not being able to successfully commit Grey to a drug and alcohol rehabilitation program, I filed a complaint against Judge Alexander. I soon discovered others had filed complaints about him too. He was convicted and appealed to the Supreme Court. They were getting ready to convict him again when, ironically, he died of an overdose of pills.

I filed a complaint against another judge who had perverted the legal system in my case. When the complaint was delivered to his desk he died of a heart attack. Two of the judges resigned from my case. The judge who finally heard my case and ruled to give everything to my children was indicted for attempted murder of his secretary and lover. He is out of the judicial system today.

Because God had delivered me from bitterness and I did

my best to walk in forgiveness, I took no pleasure in these events. It was often grievous to me that these people had become so corrupt that they continued to act illegally, immorally, and unethically. And if they came against me, they had to deal with my prayers and the prayers of all who were standing with me.

God took such good care of us. One day Robert was driving to Warren County to file a motion for me. It had to be recorded before a certain time, but it was snowing. The highway from Jackson to Vicksburg is hilly when it gets to Bovina, which is just past Flowers Interchange. People were sliding everywhere. His car swung around into the median strip and got stuck in the snow.

Robert thought, *Well, I've got to get this to the courthouse before the deadline.* But he didn't panic. He just sat there. He looked in his rearview mirror, and a wrecker just happened to come up behind him. The driver jumped out and said, "Want me to help you?"

Robert said, "Yes sir. I'm trying to get to Vicksburg to put something in the court records."

He said, "Well, I'll help you out." He hooked the car up and pulled it out. Robert had ten dollars in his pocket. He went to thank the man and give him the ten dollars, but when he turned around, the man was already helping another stranded person across the road. Robert got to the courthouse on time, and the papers were recorded.

During the time we spent in that tacky apartment, my soul began to be healed and restored in so many ways. I began to attend All Saints' Episcopal Church with some friends, and the priest fed me God's Word and cared for me as a shepherd should. He and his wife and their small congregation loved me back to a sense of worth. It was better than the time I had spent with Aunt Gladys in her Episcopal church years before, because this time I really knew God and loved Him so.

One night I called my friend Dean and said, "Are you ready to go?"

She said, "Yes. When are you coming?"

"I'll be right there. I'll just blow the horn," I answered.

Minutes later we were on our way to All Saints'. Dean asked, "Where are we going?" I told her and she said, "But it's Monday. Bible Study is on Tuesday."

"Oh no," I moaned in disappointment. "It's the wrong night."

"Well, it's the wrong night, but it's the right place. Let's keep going. We must need to be there," she said.

We spent a glorious time in prayer in the chapel. What joy and peace were imparted to me that night! These were the precious times that gave me the strength and courage to go on, and in the end they far outweighed any tragedy I endured.

CHAPTER 21

JUDICIAL FOOLISHNESS

My divorce case was a tangled web of good-ol'-boy judicial proceedings. In essence, Grey and his attorneys tried to convince me and several judges ruled that two-thirds of my life was worth nothing, and I refused to accept that. Few wives in Mississippi during that time bucked the system as I did. It is amusing to me that when I sought help from the ACLU, I was turned down. I went to the library to look up organizations for women. I called NOW and was told that at that time they had limited resources and were helping lesbians, so they could not help me. Because I was not black, a lesbian, or an unwed mother I was on my own.

In the back of this book I give a chronological description of the case. It does not include every legal motion and pleading, but it does provide enough information to reveal the legal wrangling I experienced. I insert personal facts to give a clear picture of how all the aspects of my life fit together in the timeline.

At first I spent a lot of hard-earned money on attorneys who produced no results, primarily because nearly every lawyer in our area was connected to Grey or obligated to him in some way. All but two of my lawyers wanted me to settle for a small fraction of what was rightfully mine and did not want to take the case to court and oppose Grey Flowers. The first attorney who was willing to fight for me was Martha Gerald, the attorney I hired when Grey first told me he was going to divorce me. But because he paid her fee when we reconciled, she was legally prohibited from representing me later. The second attorney who fought for me was the last one I hired, and it obviously took me a long time to find him. Needless to say, finding an attorney who had the courage to buck the system and fight for me was one of the greatest challenges in this long ordeal.

Most of the time I had to represent myself, or go *pro se*. I spent a lot of time in the law library, trying to find cases to support what I knew was right and learn as much about judicial procedure as possible. I read Sheldon's, *Divorce and Alimony* and the Mississippi College Law Library in Jackson proved invaluable. I read all the divorce cases I could, and the law librarians were always helpful. I read the Canon Laws of Mississippi from the Mississippi Judicial Committee. I wrote many of the motions and briefs myself. When I went to the Supreme Court of Mississippi Law Library to became familiar with the chancery courts in Hinds and Warren counties, I also found out the power of their clerks.

After that I made it a point to find out that the clerk in Hinds County was very cooperative, but the clerk of Warren County was not. I also discovered that the clerk of Warren County was the highest paid official in Mississippi, receiving more money than the governor. Then I realized that the clerk's son was the attorney for the bank that held the loan on Ceres

Plantation, and that the clerk's wife was the acting tax assessor for Warren County. These three people had powerful access and control. It was then that I discovered how records in my case were moved about and altered so easily.

Although court records are public, I had considerable trouble obtaining mine. Once I was in the records room in Warren County doing some research on my case. I was ushered into the clerk's office, the door was shut, and the clerk asked me to sit down. The files in my hands were taken from me, and he told me that I did not have access to them. I told him that I was acting *pro se*, and he said, "Go home." I had to go to the State Supreme Court to see my own case records, but Grey and his attorneys had access to everything. It was during this time that I found proof that the records had been changed from Hinds County to Warren County, as Hinds County was not the legal jurisdiction for our divorce case. The issue of jurisdiction was significant in my case because my brother-in-law, Judge Nat Bullard, was the presiding judge in Warren County.

On one occasion when I represented myself, the attorney who had previously been my counsel refused to give me my records unless I paid him $1,000.00 more—or so his secretary insisted. I left his office distraught, only to find I had a parking ticket. My dime had not gone far enough. I had a cast on one arm because I had slipped on the ice and broken my wrist a few days before. To add injury to insult, I slipped again and fell into a pothole, skinning my knees, shredding my stockings, and scraping my other arm. Now I was crying.

I managed to get up, grab the ticket, and drive to the nearby police station to pay it. Limping, dirty, and tattered, I was quite a sight! A couple of officers immediately surrounded me and asked if they could help me. Through my tears I explained my situation. As they escorted me to a room that had barred windows and people standing about, all eyes were on me. I was sure everyone was wondering what terrible crime I had committed!

One officer said, "Do you see that lady over there with the pretty white hair?"

"Yes, I see her," I sobbed.

"Well, that's who you'll have to talk to." The other officer called the woman and she came over to get me. She was stern.

"What's wrong?" she asked.

I blurted out my sad story of the parking ticket, the pothole, and the lawyer. "They say it doesn't make any difference that you have been married thirty-four years, had nine pregnancies, raised seven children, been faithful to your husband—you still don't get any alimony!"

I had really lost my cool by that time.

"Why?" she seemed suddenly interested.

"Because my husband is also a lawyer, and so nobody will help me. I don't know what else to do, and now I've got this ticket . . ."

"Give me that ticket," she said forcefully, taking it out of my hand and tearing it up. "You keep on fighting. I gave up too soon. Mine was also a lawyer. Why do you think I'm working behind this cage every day? Mine took twenty years of my life and then wanted his secretary. Damn it, you keep on going!" Her stern face had turned angry. I promised her I would continue fighting, and we talked about how we hoped that some day the marital laws would become more just.

Of course, she was not the only woman I had encountered who had a story similar to mine. My acquaintance with the Capital Investors Club wives and other women friends in the South whose husbands had divorced them and left them with next to nothing was too common. It was truly a man's world. The next day, a male friend of mine went with me to the attorney's office and demanded that the secretary release my files to me. She did it without hesitation and made no mention of the $1,000. (I rest my case!)

In general, fair play, honesty, and integrity were not part of the judicial proceedings of my divorce case. I soon learned that either Robert or I needed to check the docket every day because Grey's attorneys would file motions and not notify me or my attorney, if I had one. However, there were a few rare, funny moments. Like the time one of my attorneys showed up at court having had a few too many drinks. He went to the restroom and came back with his shirttail caught in the zipper of his pants! He said to me, "There is going to be a divorce today and I don't care who gets it."

I said, "Well I care who gets it and who gets what!"

Then things turned ugly. Loudly, so my friends could hear, he yelled, "Well, I don't! Get into the courtroom and sit down. I'm going into chambers and meet with the judge. We're getting this over today." When he returned from the judge's chambers, he leaned over and said, "Judge Moss wants to hear only testimony of the last three years and will only allow Mr. Flowers to testify."

This was so ridiculous that I could only blurt out, "But we've been separated for nearly three years. How can he testify about that?"

"That doesn't matter," he said emphatically. "That's all he wants to hear."

Soon it was evident that a deal had been made behind my back. Grey made carefully rehearsed accusations that were completely contrary to his previous deposition, given under oath. My lawyer remained silent and disputed nothing. The next day I fired him, and Grey's attorneys disputed my right to fire him and represent myself. When I appealed to the Supreme Court of Mississippi, they upheld the lower court's ruling that I had to retain this attorney and I could not represent myself!

I appealed to the governor, which also brought no results because Grey was good friends with the lieutenant governor and the governor was out of the country. Eventually, however, my attorney wanted to quit my case and filed against everyone himself, so the court allowed me to dismiss him and go *pro se*.

While representing myself, I wanted to call Judge Moss to the stand to show his connections with Grey and Judge Bullard and therefore prove conflict of interest. I subpoenaed him, and as he was the presiding judge in the case, he was present when I called him to the stand.

"I'm not thinking of taking the stand," he said, very angry now.

"Your Honor, a subpoena to appear has been issued to

you," I said.

"All right, Bailiff. Come over and swear me in," he fumed.

"Will Your Honor take the stand, please?" I insisted.

"I will not! I'm the judge, and I'll sit here!"

I pulled out the Canon Laws of the Judges and read the law that stated that a judge may not sit in judgment when he is subpoenaed to appear as a witness. Then I suggested that he recuse himself.

"This is my court and I will do what I want!" he bellowed. That was the voice of judicial corruption speaking loud and clear to anyone who had ears to hear. He adamantly refused to step down. I did not question him or anyone else that day, as other witnesses I had subpoenaed (my estranged children) had not shown up. No one was held in contempt of court or censored.

Then Grey's attorneys called me to the stand and they all proceeded to try to humiliate me. Grey was present, and it was so outrageous that even he became upset at how I was being treated. At one point his attorney had to restrain him when he protested. Although I felt like I was being crushed by a bulldozer, I saw that at least for that one moment, Grey realized the truth of what he had set in motion when he declared that he would destroy me. He sat and wept as his attorneys tore my life apart. But it was too late, he was too sick, and I believe he felt helpless to stop it.

The sixteen years I persevered to receive what was rightfully mine were extremely painful and frustrating, but I know God used them to help expose a great deal of corruption and bring change. At that time there were no laws in

Mississippi to divide marital assets. Whoever the judge decided to play ball with received all or most of whatever the divorced couple had acquired together. Shortly after my case was settled another case, *Ferguson v. Ferguson,* set precedent for all other divorce proceedings with regard to the distribution of marital assets.

PROPERTY DISTRIBUTION: Mississippi is a "title" state. Each spouse retains his or her property for which they have title. There are no statutory provisions in Mississippi for considerations regarding property division. However, Mississippi has judicially adopted the "equitable division" systems of property division. Recent court decisions have allowed for a wife's contributions to the acquisition of assets to provide the court with authority to divide any jointly accumulated assets on an "equitable" basis. A 1994 case (Ferguson v. Ferguson) spelled out a set of factors for the equitable division of marital property: (1) a spouse's substantial contribution to the accumulation of property; (2) the degree to which a spouse has previously expended or disposed of any marital property; (3) the market and emotional value of the property in question; (4) the value of any non-marital or separate property; (5) the tax consequences of the division of property; (6) the extent to which property division may eliminate the need for alimony or any other future friction between the parties; (7) the needs of the party, considering income, assets, and earning capacity; and (8) any other equitable factors. [Mississippi Case Law].[1]

[1]http://www.divorcesource.com/info/divorcelaws/mississippi.shtml

Ferguson v. Ferguson was filed in 1994 and unfortunately was not in place until after my case was finished. Mississippi is still not a community property state, but at least some improvements were made.

Many people observe my tenacity to receive what was rightfully mine in my divorce settlement and see nothing but revenge; and in the beginning, when I was bitter, that was certainly a factor. But after God delivered me from bitterness and challenged me to walk in forgiveness, my heart changed. I believe God put that tenacity in me for two important reasons: first, to make a statement to all women that what they do as wives and mothers is valuable—financially as well as socially; and second, to make enough noise that good people in Mississippi would realize how corrupt the judicial system is and try to make things right.

CHAPTER 22

SIX COFFINS AND A FUNERAL

In 1990 Grey and I began to work out a fair settlement for us and for our children. After all, we had been able to come to an agreement over the sale of Ceres Plantation. We set about trying to divide the rest of our assets, including personal items, stocks, oil leases, and family heirlooms. Soon I was summoned to the Special Master's office and two of our children were present with Grey's lawyer. The children convinced the Special Master to forbid me to have any contact with Grey. This not only hurt me deeply but dashed my hopes for a fair settlement.

By this time the diabetes had taken its toll and Grey went into the hospital for kidney dialysis. He suddenly decided to rewrite his will, and the new instrument was witnessed by the ICU nurse when he signed it. Each child with the exception of Robert had made a list of the things they wanted, and these things were now designated as theirs in Grey's new will. Robert was disinherited. All of this took place before there was any legal property settlement.

Then shortly after Thanksgiving Grey fell and hit his head

while my son Craig was visiting with him. Julia's husband Terrell came over and both of these men, who are doctors, decided not to take him to the hospital. They put him in bed, and two days later he was finally taken to the hospital. He had only been there for a day or two when he died. I learned of Grey's death from Debbie, who came to my condominium to tell me. My doorbell rang, and when I opened the door she cried. "Mama, Daddy's dead. Come quick. I want you to see him before they take him away."

"Where is he?" I asked calmly.

"Baptist Hospital," she answered.

"I'll go right down," I said and hugged her. She got back into her car and left.

I called a friend and the two of us went to the hospital together. When I walked into ICU, the nurse said, "He's over there to the left." Debbie was standing beside her father's body. There was a curtain around half of the cubicle and a sheet across the lower half of his body.

I walked to the side of the bed. I looked at him and said very quietly, "Grey, I truly hope you have found the real peace that you've been searching for."

Debbie overheard me and said almost frantically, "I know he has! I know he has!"

The nurse came over and said, "You'll have to wash your hands over there before you leave. And it would be best if you left now."

I washed my hands and left ICU first, then Debbie followed. I started down the hall with my friend when a former friend of Grey's and mine came rushing up to us. He told me how sorry he was. He happened to be the broker to whom Grey had given permission to purge my stock account just before Grey had threatened to divorce me.

My friend and I walked into the hospital chapel and sat down for quite a while. I wondered what memories our children would have of Grey. I wondered where he was and if he had ever really known Jesus. I hoped he had. Finally we got up and went back to my place. That evening I got a telephone call from Craig. He said that I could come to the funeral if I sat with Betty and Ettie in the third row behind the family.

"No Craig. I don't think I'll come. I said good-bye to your father a very long time ago."

"All right," he said and hung up.

Craig also called Robert, who was in South Bend, Indiana, and offered to pay for his flight down to attend the funeral. Robert said, "Why? He's already distanced himself and disinherited me." When Grey had begun kidney dialysis, Robert had tried to see him several times the year before he died. The other children made it clear that Robert could not see their father unless one of them (and not Debbie) was present during the visit. This was completely unacceptable to Robert. However, he did telephone Grey on several occasions to tell him that he was praying for him and that he loved him.

The day after Grey died and before the funeral, the children went to the attorney's office to read the will. Our property and assets were divided among six of the seven children. I learned that Julia had called the Special Master two days before Grey's death, urging him to make a determination immediately. The Special Master's decision was filed the day after Grey's death.

His decision was identical to Grey's revised will.

Soon after Grey's funeral all of the children but Robert filed to take their father's place in the divorce proceedings, as there were still a great number of assets to be divided between Grey and me. Therefore, my children entered the divorce to oppose me. Until this happened, I never thought that it was possible. It never occurred to me that they would go this far. Now I had the horror of being divorced by my children. I knew they just wanted to make certain they didn't lose anything they had been granted in Grey's will (the remaining assets were close to a million dollars by this time), but this was the most painful time of all.

Grey's words came back to me, "I'll find some way to destroy you." I realized that his ultimate goal was not to impoverish me. He used the money to accomplish the greater heartache, which was to separate me from my children. By threatening to disinherit them and using religious doctrine of the Presbyterian Church to convince them that my leaving him was a sin, he persuaded all but Robert that I should be shunned. When he died, they immediately filed to replace him to protect their financial interests. But that was not the worst of it. They (the substituted party, as they are referred to in the following) filed a Motion to Hold Anne Flowers in Contempt of Court.

WHEREFORE, the substituted party for U. Grey Flowers, Deceased prays for the following relief:

1. That Anne Williams Flowers be held in contempt of this Court for her wilful, continued, and obstinate failure and refusal to comply with the Court's Order on Division of Marital Property pur-

suant to the parties' divorce;

2. That this Court mandate that Anne Williams Flowers immediately comply with all requirements of the Order on Division of Marital Property entered herein;

3. That Anne Williams Flowers be made to pay all costs of this proceeding, together with and including a reasonable attorney's fee;

4. That this Court enter a judgment against Anne Williams Flowers for the amount past due together with interest, and that this Court take other steps as necessary to require Anne Williams Flowers to pay the substituted party for U. Grey Flowers, Deceased, all amounts past due;

5. That Anne Williams Flowers be incarcerated in the Hinds County Jail by the Sheriff of this county until such time as she has purged herself of contempt of this Court; and

6. The substituted party for U. Grey Flowers, Deceased prays for such other relief as may be proper in the premises under these particular circumstances.

Respectfully submitted,

U. GREY FLOWERS, DECEASED

By: Jeffrey P. Hubbard, Attorney for
U. Grey Flowers, Deceased

Not only did they take Grey's place in the judicial proceedings but they actually wanted to throw me in jail! Forgiveness was one thing, but the reality of my situation now became too much to bear. My heart literally broke into a thousand pieces at the cold rejection of my children. The little girl in me, who had rocked her doll on the porch of the boarding house, dreaming of the day when she would be a mother and rock her children, cried and cried. This little girl had always wanted to be a mother like the mother she had never had, to be a grandparent like the grandparents she never knew.

The emotional pain of it all was killing me. I had to find a way to handle this. In the end, the only way I could face my children in court was to imagine them in six coffins, dead to me. I sat in my living room and envisioned I was saying goodbye to each child. Then I gently put each coffin in the ground and wept. This was the only way I could get closure and keep going. I told God, "You know how I love them. If I can have them back, it will be up to you. You're the one in the resurrection business, not I." Just knowing they were in His hands gave me a tremendous peace.

After I did this, I found I could remember our good times together with joy instead of overwhelming sorrow. When I walked into court to battle them over their latest motion, Ella was by my side. She was such a great support. I will never forget as she accompanied me into the courtroom and we passed the children. She pointed her finger at them as a mother would and said, "You ought to be ashamed of yourselves! You know better than this. I never taught you this kind of behavior." I think they knew she was right, and they loved and respected Ella, but they were too afraid of losing their inheritance from their father. He and the lawyer had obviously convinced them that I would take everything for myself if I won. The truth is that I would never have denied them anything they wanted or needed if I could provide it.

In 1996 the children (and Grey posthumously) won nearly everything. The court declared that the $208,000 I had received from the sale of the plantation was all that was due to me. Furthermore, I was to turn over some of my wedding gifts, inherited items, and other keepsakes and valuables to the children. In other words, the judge honored Grey's recently revised will over the agreement he had signed and filed in the courthouse sixteen years earlier as part of our reconciliation after his first threat to divorce me.

A poignant moment that epitomizes my sorrow happened shortly after I had turned many of my possessions over to the children. I received a box in the mail from Julia. Inside were the bronzed baby shoes of each one of my children. The enclosed note said simply, "Mother, these are yours." I recalled my mother's story of saying goodbye to me as a baby, my tiny feet sticking out from the blanket, the image that haunted her for years.

I realized that I was the only one who knew which shoe belonged to which child. A friend was with me as I identified them. She said, "A mother never forgets her children."

CHAPTER 23

SAYING GOOD-BYE TO THE PAST

The wonderful thing about knowing the Lord and being a part of the body of Christ is having a family. When my own family turned away from me and when my father passed away, God provided other fathers and mothers, other children and grandchildren, and other brothers and sisters. I was surrounded by good Christian friends, great people who never let me feel sorry for myself and reminded me of all the things I had to be thankful for. I am especially grateful to my friend Dean Alexander, who walked every step of the way with me and helped me say good-bye to my past.

Grey's Final Resting Place

Something happened about three years after Grey's death that was both sad and hilarious at the same time—one of those situations where all you can do is laugh because it is so ridiculously sad. I felt impressed to visit his gravesite. I had not attended his funeral, and I was curious to know where our children had laid him to rest. I went to the cemetery office and used the name Helen Bounds, saying, "I was not here for the funeral, and I would just like to see where Grey

Flowers was buried."

They looked him up in the files, got a map out, and put an "X" where he was located. Then they said, "Now, the pavement will stop at this point. Just continue on the dirt road until it dead-ends. Take a left and drive back the other side. On your right-hand side you will see a gnarled pear tree with a birdhouse that has a little hole in it. Park the car, walk toward the tree, and then face northwest. Walk about thirty feet from the pear tree and you'll see a plaque on the ground."

"Thank you," I said, a little confused. I then proceeded to follow their instructions. Indeed, it was like being on a primitive treasure hunt in the woods. I had to be careful where I was walking because there were cow patties all over the place. They had buried Grey in an isolated pasture with nothing but a small, bronze plaque marking the grave. It gave his name, date of birth, date of death, and the final line said, "U.S. Marines" (actually, he was only in the Marines for two or three months before he was asked to leave).

I was exhausted from the hunt and stood there in shock. I went back to the cemetery office and asked, "Why didn't they bury him down where those beautiful live oak trees are and the grass is green and well-kempt?"

The man looked at me stonily and said, "It cost more money. This is an area that we will eventually develop."

I said, "Are you going to pave the road?"

He answered, "Yes, we will eventually."

I went directly to Dean's to tell her about my adventure. She was aghast. Then, when we realized the irony of it all, we had one of the biggest laughs in years. It was therapeutic.

Six weeks later on a beautiful Sunday, I called another friend of mine who knew little of my divorce case. I asked her if she would like to go for a ride, and she said yes. I picked her up and as we rode I said, "Did you go to Grey's graveside service?"

She said, "No, but I went to the funeral."

I said, "It's so pretty. Let's go out there."

She thought that was a good idea, so on we went. When the pavement stopped and we hit the gravel road, she asked, "Where are you going?"

I said, "To show you the gravesite." I finally stopped the car at the pear tree. "I'll wait here. You go to the pear tree with the birdhouse, then take about thirty steps that way, and you'll see the grave."

My friend was still dressed for church and had on her high heels. I watched her stumble across the field and wondered what she was thinking. She stood at the plaque for the longest time, looked around, and then stumbled back to the car. She got inside and said angrily, "Step on it."

I went as fast as I legally could in a cemetery. We said nothing until we were half-way home. Then she opened her mouth and yelled for about ten minutes. "What were they thinking of?!! He gave them all the money! The least they could have done was put him in a proper place!" When I told her how much cheaper it was, she cried, "That's the most outrageous thing I've ever heard!"

I picked this particular friend because I knew other people would believe her. She had not been with me through the entire ordeal of the divorce like Dean had, and people would know she was not exaggerating when the story was told. And what a story it was!

Good-bye, Ettie

On Ettie's eighty-fifth birthday, when we were alone together, she shocked me by saying, "Anne Sharp, please forgive me for not protecting you. I was just a new citizen, your father was away, and the war was going on. I was afraid and I didn't know what to do."

My stomach tightened because I knew exactly what she meant. During the war our doctor was part of a group of private physicians who took care of President Roosevelt. For this reason, Ettie thought of him as a very influential man, but he was obsessed with me. He would make up excuses to see me, often took pictures of me, and on several occasions his behavior was totally inappropriate. When Daddy sent me to camp to get me out of the city for awhile, this man actually got my address at camp and wrote to me! He wrote poems about me and would quote other poems to me.

I felt very vulnerable and frightened, but with the war going on and Daddy so involved in it, I confided in Ettie when I got home from camp. She told me she could not worry my father with anything right now. The next time the doctor called and wanted to see me, she said, "He has bought a new camera and wants to take your picture today."

"Ettie, I can't do that. I just can't!" I cried.

"You have to. He's a friend of the family," she said.

"Just tell him I can't."

"I can't stop him. He's a friend of the family." she

answered. "I can't do anything."

That day I ran away to a friend's house, and Ettie had to make an excuse. This ended the doctor's fascination with me. Neither of us mentioned it again until her eighty-fifth birthday, when she asked for my forgiveness. I could tell that it gave her tremendous relief just to ask.

I said, "Ettie, I forgave you long ago. Let me tell you what happened. Years later, when Daddy was in the hospital, that doctor came to see him and asked to see me as well. I met him at a restaurant and took two of my small children with me. He asked me to forgive him, and at that point I said that I wasn't sure I could. I just didn't know how. Later, of course, I did."

Then Ettie told me about the abuses the girls at the Roman Catholic orphanage had suffered. She said that she had felt guilty all these years for not protecting me from that doctor, especially because of her own experience. I could tell that she was at peace about the matter at last. This was the beginning of God preparing me to lay both my mothers to rest.

In 1998 my mother passed away in North Carolina, near her sister Nancy, and was buried in Florida. It was hard for me, but I was so thankful to have had the time I had spent with her. Then Ettie's health became worse and worse. She had never accepted Jesus into her life, primarily because she was so wounded by the abuses she had suffered while under the authority of the Roman Catholic Church. When she married my Father, she was excommunicated because he was divorced, and so her hostility against God and church had remained throughout her life. I knew that not all Catholics were abusive, but that was her experience.

Ettie was in her nineties and dying and didn't know Jesus

when I received a telephone call from Julia, who said Ettie was in heart failure. She asked me to come get her because she didn't have a car. Immediately I drove to pick up my daughter, and we drove to Vicksburg. Even though Julia was in the car, I prayed a great deal of the time. When we got to the hospital, we walked into the emergency room and I said, "I'm Anne Flowers. Where is my mother, Mrs. Williams?"

They said, "Room 2."

I was still praying when I walked into her room, but I knew what I was to do. I felt the Holy Spirit strengthening me in a special way. I was very aware that my sister Betty and her daughter were sitting against the wall. There was also a nurse and the woman who had been taking care of Ettie. I said nothing to them and walked over to the bed. I gently put my left hand under Ettie's little head, near the back of her neck. I took my right hand and put it over her right hand. She had on an oxygen mask and was unconscious.

I said, "Ettie, I know you're deaf and blind. But I know that your spirit can hear me, and I'm talking to you. This is Anne Sharp. Listen to me. You've got to make the decision that is the most important decision of your life. It's for the rest of your life. It's for eternity. If you ever expect to see Daddy again, or if you ever want to see me again, you're going to have to make this decision. Accept Jesus as your Lord and Savior. Take Him now, before it's too late. I want you to be with us."

Ettie's blind eyes opened up and she became conscious. She tried to smile under the oxygen mask and her eyes shone. She said, "Yes, yes, yes." Then her eyes closed again.

I said, "Ettie, I'll hold your hand, darling. I'm right here.

I'm right here. Now you can let go."

I stood for what seemed like the longest time, holding her hand. Out of the corner of my eye I observed something very curious. Julia started toward the foot of the bed, stopped abruptly, and then suddenly went straight back against the wall. Then the woman who had been taking care of Ettie did the same thing. The nurse, my sister, and her daughter never moved.

After awhile I let go of Ettie's hand and moved away from the bed. I watched as Julia and the caregiver were now able to come near the bed. Then I left. Ettie died just a few hours later without regaining consciousness. God had given me a great gift and I was ever so thankful and relieved. She was buried next to my father at Cedar Grove Plantation, where they were married, and I rejoiced because she went to heaven.

CHAPTER 24

SUNSET

After my natural mother's death in 1998, I started what I call my Noah's Ark Experience. I just began packing all my things. I knew I was leaving Jackson. I just didn't know where I was going. People would come by and ask why I had so many boxes. I would say, "Well, I'm moving."

"Where are you moving?"

I'd say, "I'm not sure."

As I packed I remembered something that had happened in 1986. I had gone to San Destin, Florida, with two good Christian friends for a much-needed vacation. One morning I got up early and went for a walk on the beach. Anybody who knows me is aware that I don't like to walk. I prefer to get in the car to go next door! But I began to walk on the beach in obedience to the Lord, who had told me to do so. I walked east, toward the sunrise. It was still dark out, but you could see the sun beginning to come up. Walking in the sand was really difficult for me, but I walked and walked and walked.

Finally I said, "Lord, can I turn around?"

He said, "No. Keep going." So I kept going and kept going and I was really having a hard time doing it. All the while my mind was thinking about the difficulties of the divorce, everything that was either a torment or grievance in my life at that time.

I was really huffing and puffing and said again, "Can I turn around now?"

He said, "No. I'll tell you when." So I kept going. After what seemed to be an eternity, He finally said, "Turn around."

I stopped and turned around. Breathing hard, I looked toward the hotel. I thought, *I'll never make it. It's too far away. I'm exhausted and I'm out on this beach alone. How can I get to that hotel?*

He said, "Just start walking." So I started walking and kept walking, and suddenly it got a bit easier. Pretty soon I was picking up a stride I'd never experienced in my life. I was walking and I was full of joy. I was getting close to the hotel when I heard Him say, "Look."

I looked at the western clouds and saw a reflection of the sun coming up in the East. It was beautiful. I marveled at it and said out loud, "Ohhhhhh."

He said, "You see? This is like the sunset of your life. I am going to make it easy for you."

Jesus' words proved so true. After Ettie died, I felt that my time in Jackson was finished, and for some time Tulsa, Oklahoma, had been on my heart. After World War II my father had taken me there. He was designing the first self-contained trailer for Spartan Manufacturing Company. We stayed at the Mayo Hotel for several months, and I fell in love with this wonderful city. Then Robert lived there for a while, and I had visited him a couple of times. I still found the city warm, friendly, and a beautiful place to live. So I got on the Internet and located an apartment there. I leased it and some furniture for three months. In this way, I would "test the waters" and see if this was where I was really supposed to go.

During the second month in Tulsa, my daughter Elizabeth called and asked me to visit her and her family in Switzerland, where they were living at the time. I accepted the invitation gladly, cancelled the rest of my apartment lease in Tulsa, drove back to Jackson, and flew to Switzerland. We spent three wonderful weeks together.

One evening Elizabeth and I were sitting in my hotel room, just the two of us, talking into the wee hours of the morning. She asked me questions about her father, about our marriage, and about the divorce. Finally she looked at me with her big, blue eyes and said, "You're not bitter."

I said, "No, I'm not. I've really been blessed."

Her lovely eyes filled with tears and spilled over. She said, "Can you ever forgive me?"

I said, "Darling, I already have."

We hugged and she said, "I've been so selfish. I've just been looking after my own family."

I said, "That's what you should be doing." I chuckled because her tummy was swollen with her ninth child.

After I returned to Jackson, I sat in my living room one evening with the lights off and looked through the windows into the garden. I said out loud, "Anne Sharp, you're never coming back to this place. Never." I now knew I was to move to Tulsa immediately. Tulsa is west of Jackson, of course, just like Jesus showed me fifteen years earlier on the beach in Florida.

At this writing I live in a beautiful house in Tulsa. I have made wonderful friends here. My daughter Elizabeth and her family moved here after September 11, 2001, and live just a few miles away. God has also done a miracle in my daughter Debbie, whom we now call Deborah because she is so changed. After being addicted to drugs and alcohol in her young years, she became completely free of any addictions. She now has a masters degree in psychology and has become a Christian. We have spent wonderful times together, and she is delightful to be around. She laughs about the fact that she thinks we are so much alike!

If that wasn't enough, at this writing and just recently my son Al and his family have moved to Tulsa as well! Now I'm enjoying more grandchildren every day than I could ever have imagined. They are all such blessings to me. I do have some contact with a few of my other grandchildren, who are also absolutely wonderful.

My God is the God of resurrection. He restored my soul. And just as He promised that day on the beach, He gave me His peace, prosperity, and joy in the sunset of my life. He took me from riches to rags to Jesus, the only true riches.

APPENDIX I

CHRONOLOGY OF EVENTS

1951

Uriah Grey Flowers and Anne Sharp Williams are married in Vicksburg, Mississippi.

1952

Our first son, Grey, is born in Vicksburg.

1953

We move to Jackson, Mississippi.

1954

Ella comes to work for us full time.

1959

Grey contracts viral equine encephalitis.

He is later diagnosed with diabetes. Doctors order him to quit smoking and drinking, but he does not.

I attend my grandmother's funeral, see my aunt and mother, am puzzled by Grey's behavior.

1966

My father, A. R. Williams, dies. Grey and Judge Nat Bullard (my sister's husband) become co-trustees of the A. R. Williams Trust.

Grey uses some of my inheritance to buy the land and build the house near the country club.

1967

I am diagnosed with cervical cancer and have a hysterectomy.

Grey purchases oil leases with my inheritance checks.

1979

Grey sells our country club home in Jackson, we move into several condominiums. He uses the full equity of $100,000.00 from the sale of the home and obtains a loan of $200,000.00 to remodel Ceres Plantation to accommodate our family.

1980

We move to Ceres Plantation and our second son, Craig, a doctor, marries.

1981

Our first daughter, Julia, marries Dr. Terrel Williams. Grey decides to turn Ceres Plantation into a working farm and incurs almost another million dollars in debt, including the purchase of $500,000.00 in farm equipment.

1982

January

I refuse to sign my father's trust check over to Grey because I am concerned that Grey will misuse the money. I tell him I am going to save it for Robert and Debbie's education.

February   Grey tells me he's going to divorce me, and I will get nothing. He begins to spread rumors to our grown children and others in the community that I am unstable.

May   Grey tells me that he has told Thomas Crockett, his legal counsel, to go ahead and file divorce papers against me.

September   Robert enters The McCallie School and escapes the plantation.

November   Debbie enters All Saints' in Vicksburg and begins smoking and using drugs and alcohol.

Grey has not filed against me, and I am not sure if he has lied to me or changed his mind. To be safe, I obtain Martha Gerald as legal counsel. She begins an investigation of Grey's financial assets.

1983

March   At my request the Presbyterian Church refers us to a "Christian" counselor. Grey and I go together several times, then separately, then I continue by myself. Debbie is also seeing a counselor.

June   Grey tells me he will not seek a divorce if I will stop my attorney's investigation. I confront him with spreading rumors that I am unstable and he says he is sorry. He will pay my attorneys' fee, and as a show of good faith he will put the plantation home and 2.88 acres of the land in my name alone. I agree. The home is put in my name, and we go on a second honeymoon, which isn't so grand.

August 4   Grey writes a letter to the children that he has put

	the house and 2.88 acres of Ceres Plantation in my name to correct the wrongs he has done me over the years.
October	Grey threatens to destroy me, so I leave the plantation, taking Debbie with me. Grey agrees to sign my apartment lease and support us for six months.

1984

	Grey shuts down the Ceres Plantation farming operation and sells the equipment at auction for $225,000.00.
January	Our third son, Al, elopes.
March 11	Debbie attempts suicide the first time.
July	Two of Grey's friends, Robert, and I attempt to commit Grey to a drug and alcohol rehabilitation program. We are unsuccessful because of collusion between Judge Alexander, Grey, and my brother-in-law, Judge Nat Bullard.
October 25	Grey paid Martha Gerald my fee, so she cannot be my attorney because it would be a conflict of interest. I realize Grey tricked me. I contact another attorney, Mark Chinn. I (plaintiff) file a Complaint and ask for separate maintenance, child support, and custody.
October 29	Grey files for additional time to answer.
November 2	Grey files for more additional time to answer.
November 7	Mark Chinn sends interrogatories to Grey, including an accounting of my father's trust. Grey requests more time to answer.

1985

January 11	Mark Chinn files Amended Complaint.

January 18	Grey answers original October 25th Complaint.
February	I find a lump in my left breast, which is diagnosed malignant.
May 25	Our second daughter Elizabeth is married, and I am only a guest. Ettie, my sister, and brother-in-law plan the wedding. Grey agrees to pay for my dress if it is under $100. My children (except for Robert) have now ceased contact with me.
May 27	Mark Chinn files interrogatories to Grey again.
June 17	Judge Bullard (my brother-in-law) recuses himself from our case and appoints Judge Joe Moss in Hinds County (Jackson) to preside.
June 24	Deposition of Earl Lundy, Grey's banker, which discloses the loans Grey placed on Ceres Plantation for $800,000.00 and then another $100,000.00.
August	My doctor and a mammogram confirm that the lump in my breast is gone.

I file *pro se* (representing myself) in Yazoo County, where my father's trust was set up, to have my husband and brother-in-law removed as trustees, charging conflict of interest and failure to produce accounting records. My cousin agrees to act as trustee because he is handling most of my father's property.

The papers are sent to my sister and Ettie, and they refuse to cooperate. Judge Bullard and my sister go to Yazoo County and threaten John Holmes, the attorney who set up the trust. Judge Bullard tells him that Holmes and his son, who is also an attorney, will never win a case in his court again if he sides with me.

John Holmes calls me in Jackson and apologizes

for not siding with me. He says, "I'm sorry, but I have to make a living." My cousin is horrified at the outcome, but there is nothing he can do.

August 30   Chinn files Motion for Leave to Amend Plaintiff's Countermotion and Amended Counterclaim.

September 25   Chinn files Supplement to Plaintiff's Interrogatories (that Grey has not answered).

September 27   Grey files Response to Plaintiff's Interrogatories and Counterclaim.

December 6   Mark Chinn withdraws as my counsel because we have a difference of opinion on how to conduct my case. He favors a settlement of $600 a month for five years only and refuses to take the case to trial. I believe he is being influenced by Grey.

December 12   Trial date set by Judge Moss in Hinds County and I am without counsel.

1986

January   After repeated attempts to find an attorney who has no ties or relationship with Grey, I hire L. C. James. I find out by accident that Grey's attorney, Thomas Crockett, refiled for an automatic divorce from me on the grounds of desertion in the same court (Hinds County) and Mark Chinn had never countered the complaint. To disprove this allegation, Robert and I return to the plantation to live.

January 11   Grey has his attorney issue a restraining order to remove Robert and me from the plantation. Two deputies arrest us the second night we are there, but we are allowed to go back to the apartment in Jackson. We are ordered never to go to the plantation again. However, this short stay negated Grey's automatic divorce on grounds of desertion.

March	L. C. James reviews my case and refuses to go to trial.
April	Grey files Motion of Limene to prohibit me from representing myself, but I appear *pro se*.
May	I hire Robert Marshall to represent me.
June	My motion in Yazoo County to have Grey and Judge Bullard dismissed as co-trustees of my father's trust is denied. The judge states that he does not believe it is a conflict of interest.

Hearing of Divorce in Hinds County by Judge Moss is concluded with no decision. He says he will render his opinion in ten days, but he does not. Grey's deposition is his only testimony. He sends a picture of himself in a hospital gown saying that he is unable to appear. Our new son-in-law, Dr. Terrel Williams testifies that Grey has a terminal illness and will probably not live more than two or three months. (Grey did not die until four and a half years later.)

September   Judge Moss reopens the divorce case in Jackson at Grey's request (he has recovered from terminal illness) and over (my attorney) Robert Marshall's objection. Judge Moss allows Grey to testify again, in person, even though he had previously submitted his deposition as his testimony and the case had been concluded.

Grey testifies that he is nearly bankrupt and charges me with habitual cruel and inhuman treatment because I attempted to commit him to a drug and alcohol rehabilitation program. His testimony is limited to the last three years, but I had not lived with him but six months during that time. He would not allow me to cross-examine Grey.

Judge Moss does not render an opinion in the courtroom, but the docket shows a two-page opinion of the Court filed in Warren County immediately after the case was concluded in Hinds County. I find out because I check the dockets of each court every day.

October 20   Judgment of Divorce is handed down and filed, but my attorney and I are not notified. Again, I find out by checking the docket. The divorce decree does not dispose of marital assets.

November   I appeal to the Supreme Court of Mississippi with Robert Marshall as counsel because no settlement of property has been made in the Final Judgment of Divorce. All Judge Moss decided was that our marriage was dissolved on grounds of cruel and inhuman treatment on my part.

December   Grey sells the plantation for $1,800,000.00 even though the house and 2.88 acres, valued at $625,000.00, are in my name. $1,112,106.36 in debts and taxes are paid, leaving an equity of $677,893.64. Grey and I sign an agreement that I will receive $208,000.00 of that equity. No other marital assets are discussed at that time. Grey divides the rest of the equity among our children, excluding Robert. If I had maintained my claim on the property in my name and sold it, after taxes and debts owed I would have received $320,000.00.

1987

January   Robert Marshall decides he wants to quit law practice, so I apply for an extension of time *pro se*. Marshall requests Supreme Court's permission to resign as my attorney.

218

February	Grey petitions the Court to refuse Marshall's request to resign as my attorney.
March 13	The Supreme Court refuses Marshall's request to resign as my attorney.
March 26	Grey files a petition in the Chancery Court in Vicksburg, Warren County (so Judge Bullard will send it back to Judge Moss in Hinds County, Jackson) to remove all furniture and personal belongings from the plantation and put them in storage. I appear *pro se* and request a division of property from Judge Moss. I am refused. I point out that my case is pending in the Supreme Court and all other proceedings should be stayed by law. I am refused again.
April 5	I appear *pro se* before the Supreme Court and plead for a cease and desist in Chancery Court proceedings, which are illegal, as well as for Marshall to resign as my attorney and for me to receive a just property settlement; especially with regard to my father's trust, the sale of the plantation, and personal belongings and furniture. Soon after my motion is denied.
April 21	Grey petitions Chancery Court to avoid paying me my part of the sale of the plantation or relinquishing any furniture or personal belongings from it. I appear *pro se*. Judge Moss signs Order allowing Grey to remove furniture and personal belongings from the plantation. Nothing else is ruled upon.
May 5	I file another motion in Supreme Court to let Marshall resign and for the Chancery Court to cease and desist. Marshall files motion to withdraw as my counsel and threatens to sue all the justices, stating that I have right to act *pro se*.

May 6   Marshall's motion to withdraw is granted, but there is no decision regarding my motion for the Chancery Court to cease and desist.

May 21   Chancery Court denies my motion to set aside certain furniture and personal belongings.

June 6   I am granted more time to file my appeal *pro se* in Supreme Court. I am spending a lot of time in the law library researching and preparing my case.

June 15   I again appear *pro se* in Supreme Court and ask them to order the Chancery Court to cease and desist from any action, citing extreme circumstances.

June 16   The Chancery Court enters an Order giving the parties ten days to reach an agreement as to the division of marital property. If that is not accomplished, a special commissioner will be appointed. We do not reach an agreement and a Special Master is appointed. Later he states that he was instructed to limit his work to household items and not to deal with mineral rights, life insurance policies, pension plans, or other financial holdings. Much litigation and dispute follows the findings of this Special Master over the next few years.

June 22   The Supreme Court enters Order on Motion to Stay All Hearings in the Chancery Court. My motion is granted at last.

1988

March 11   Grey's testimony concerning our attempt to commit him to a drug and alcohol rehabilitation program revealed the collusion between himself and Judges Bullard and Alexander. I file a complaint with the Mississippi Commission on Judicial Performance alleging collusion between Judges Bullard and Alexander and Grey Flowers to illegally rescind the Order committing Grey to a drug and alcohol treatment center. I state that their illegal act prohibited Grey from receiving the help he needed, put my son and me in physical danger, caused division between me and my other children, and ultimately caused the family to be torn apart.

September   Supreme Court denies my appeal and sends the divorce case back to Judge Bullard's Chancery Court of Warren County in Vicksburg.

November   Grey's lawyers file a motion to divide personal property and furniture in Hinds County. I file a Motion to Dismiss because of lack of proper jurisdiction in Hinds County. Judge Dillard enters Order of Dismissal for lack of jurisdiction in his court.

1989

February   I file Motion Rule 60(b) to be relieved of Final Judgment filed by Judge Moss in Hinds County, citing lack of jurisdiction.

March   Because the Supreme Court sent the case back to Judge Bullard, my brother-in-law, he again recuses himself, sends it back to Judge Moss in Hinds County, and I appeal to the governor of Mississippi.

April   I file Amended Motion 60(b) to be relieved of official judgment. Receivd instructions from the governor's counsel to petition for a new judge, someone other than Judges Moss or Bullard. I submit the list of three names in timely fashion and under the instructions of Governor Ray Mabus. I ask the court clerk if Grey and his attorney had filed their list yet, and he says no. I wait outside the court clerk's office until long past the deadline, and they never file. I leave confident that since they missed the deadline, one of my judges would be picked.

No action was taken until after the governor and his wife went to Japan with other dignitaries to negotiate a trade agreement, and Grey contacted the Lt. Gov. who was an old friend of his. The Lt. Gov. reassigned Judge Moss to the case. This was a great discouragement for me.

When Governor Mabus and his wife Julie returned, I went to the governor's mansion and showed Julie the case. She said, "This is wrong. I'll speak to Ray and see what he can do." I received a call two days later and Julie's voice was strained. She apologized profusely and said, "I don't know what's happened. There's nothing I can do. I know it's wrong. You are up against a powerhouse." After Mabus was governor he was appointed ambassador to Saudi Arabia by Bill Clinton. Later on he and Julie were divorced.

1990

Grey and I begin to work out a fair settlement for us and for our children. I am summoned to the Special Master's office and two of our children are present with Grey's lawyer. They convince the Special Master to forbid me to have any contact with Grey.

The diabetes is taking its toll and Grey goes into the hospital for kidney dialysis. He suddenly rewrites his will, which is witnessed by the ICU nurse when he signs it. Each child had made a list of the items they wanted, and these things are included in the new will. Robert is disinherited.

Shortly after Thanksgiving Grey falls and hits his head. Two days later his son and son-in-law take him to the hospital. The day after Grey dies, the children go to the attorney's office to read the will. Our property and assets are divided among six of the seven children.

Date ?

The day after Grey dies all of my children except Robert file to take their father's place in the divorce.

I learn that one of my children called the Special Master two days before Grey's death, urging him to make a determination immediately. The Special Master's decision was filed just after Grey's death. His decision was nearly identical to Grey's will.

1991

June 11
I am ordered to turn over many of my personal belongings so that they can be distributed among the six children, and many of my wedding gifts from my friends and family are also distributed among them. I am also ordered to pay all court costs and attorneys fees for U. Grey Flowers concerning this motion. And, "that Anne Williams Flowers be incarcerated in the Hinds County Jail by the sheriff of this county until such time as she has purged herself of contempt of this Court."

June
I learn that Grey had begun distributing our property to the six children in 1986, and the Special Master's decision stated that these properties should remain where they were.

I decide to file against the estate and contest the Special Master's decision only because the six children have omitted their brother, Robert. If they had included him, I would have let the decision stand.

Judge Nat Bullard is reviewing a motion at his desk and dies. Braddock takes his place as Chancery Judge of Warren County.

Paul Neville becomes my attorney. He is young but honest, reliable, and courageous. Before they can put me in jail, Moss recuses himself and admits never having jurisdiction. Paul obtains what I and none of my previous attorneys were able to obtain: all of Grey's financial records, including tax returns and the distribution of my father's trust. There were joint returns filed after our separation that I had never seen or signed, among other questionable actions. He uncovers all the oil and gas leases, real estate holdings, and other holdings that were bought partially with my inheritance from my father. These holdings were distributed among our six children. He finds that Grey "neglected" to record the oil land deeds until 1988, after our separation and divorce, at which time he put them in his name.

July 5   Special Chancellor Braddock appointed by the governor says he has no constitutional power to proceed and remands the cause (division of marital assets) to the Chancery Court of Warren County.

1992

March 13   Chancery court of Warren county appoints Hon. Gerald Hoseman as Special Chancellor.

April 13	Hoseman denies the children's Motion to Dismiss and allows the filing of my Second Amended Complaint.
April 17	My Second Amended Complaint is filed.
July 7	The children's attorneys file Answer to my Second Amended Complaint.

1993

| March 1 | Trial in Chancery Court of Warren County. David May, CPA for my father and Grey, testifies that I contributed 16 to 25 percent of the marital assets; the court later finds I contributed 20 to 25 percent. We are not allowed to cross-examine him with regard to Grey's disastrous mishandling of our marital assets concerning Ceres Plantation and the farming operation. It is undisputed that had my contributions been kept separate and allowed to accumulate, they would have totaled $380,000.00 in 1986, when the divorce was granted, and $660,000.00 at the present trial. The six children and Grey's attorney assert that nothing more is owed to me, contradicting previous testimony by Grey himself when he was alive that we had only settled the issue of Ceres Plantation and had not settled with regard to mineral, stock, and cash holdings. |
| June 25 | The Chancery Court entered its Amended Opinion deciding the case and on July 6 a Final Judgment is entered by the lower court. They decide that I hold no interest in the mineral, stock, and cash holdings, much of which were purchased using my inheritance and totaled over $200,000.00 at the time of the divorce decree in 1986. The court maintains that my share of the |

marital assets was fully satisfied in the
$208,000.00 that I received from the sale of Ceres
Plantation.

July 13   I appeal the June 25th Final Judgment.

1994

January 19   Neville files a comprehensive brief giving the fol-
                 lowing Statement of the Issues (quoted below):

1. The trial court in upholding the claim of the Estate of
U. Grey Flowers, et al., that all of the marital assets had
been settled between the parties by virtue of an agreement on December 3, 1986, allowed a fraud to be perpe-
trated on the Court.

2. There is no evidence in this record that the agreement
of December 3, 1986, settled the status of any marital
asset other than the disposition of the proceeds from the
sale of Ceres Plantation, and all of the sworn testimony
in this record supports only the finding that that settlement was limited to the proceeds of the Ceres sale. The
Special Chancellor was in manifest error and without
any evidence to support his contrary finding.

3. The trial court erred under the law of the State of
Mississippi in ruling that it was unable to consider the
monetary contributions of Anne Williams Flowers to the
marital assets in the absence of the ability to award
alimony.

4. The trial court erred in refusing to allow Anne
Williams Flowers to cross-examine the expert witness of
the appellees on his conclusions concerning the contributions of the marital partners to the financial assets of
the marriage in the area of the actions of U. Grey
Flowers in causing the disastrous losses from the farm-
ing operations commenced in his declining years.

5. The trial court was manifestly in error in omitting from its calculation of the gross value of the marital estate at the time of divorce $108,954.81 in common stock holdings and $18,164.00 in cash holdings in the possession of U. Grey Flowers, all of which had been accumulated during the marriage and were not disputed.

1996

My appeal concerning the distribution of marital assets is denied at the Mississippi State Court of Appeals. Paul Neville is shocked at the decision. He tells me that the law was on our side, but we just didn't have the judges.

Appendix II

Code of Judicial Conduct Adopted by Mississippi Conference of Judges, October 25, 1974

1. A judge should uphold the integrity and independence of the judiciary.

2. A judge should avoid impropriety and the appearance of impropriety in all his activities.

3. A judge should perform the duties of his office impartially and diligently.

4. A judge may engage in activities to improve the law, the legal system, and the administration of justice.

5. A judge should regulate his extra-judicial activities to minimize the risk of conflict with his judicial duties.

6. A judge should regularly file reports of compensation received for quasi-judicial and extra-judicial activities.

7. A judge should refrain from political activity inappropriate to his judicial office.